beloved waters

beloved waters

by Paul Ford
Illustrations by Jerry Ellis

Frank Amato
PORTLAND

For Mary Ann
Who chuckles and sends me off
with a cup of java

Frank Amato Publications, Inc.

P.O. Box 82112, Portland, Oregon 97282

503.653.8108 • www.amatobooks.com

Deluxe Limited Edition issued in 2000.

Illustrations by Jerry Ellis

Cover Design by Kathy Johnson

Cover: Art Lingren casting. Frank Amato photo

Printed in Hong Kong

Softbound ISBN: 1-57188-299-5 • UPC: 0-81127-00129-3

1 3 5 7 9 10 8 6 4 2

Contents

the heart hath its reason
Of which the reason knoweth naught.
Pascal *Pensées*

Fisher's Hope

Another autumn has come with its gift of riverbound fish. My river's fishing year has begun once again—and I am filled with hope.

DAWN MIST is heavy all across the great becalmed salt marsh estuary. My boot feet churn soft black muck, and its sweet sulfurous stink delights me as I trudge shallows beneath the meandering river's grass-hummocked steep banks.

I rose very early this morning to be first on the stump pool—first to cast a bushy red and silver bucktail to mighty Chinook resting in hip-deep teak slack-water at stump's edge. Even so, another fisher well known to me arrived earlier. A Great Blue Heron, sly, stick-still, like some drear tide-carved driftpiece waits, ever-watchful, patient as the ages—a minnow will come. It has always been so and so shall it be now.

For a quarter century I have come here in the fall on minus tide mornings—forever faithful to the poetry of this place, watching for a telltale bulge, casting and casting, floating a line across and down stream, a sunk fly bottom-skipping. Skulking, crafty, always wondering, "What's below the surface? The big one? Will there be a take this morning? Yes, surely yes, on the next cast." Certainty within uncertainty.

Sometimes faith is rewarded. An almost imperceptible twitch where my leader hinges down from its lime-green fly line signals the take. Then the hook set. Leviathan's silver-black dorsal and back broach surface and the great fish is off—out of the pool and onto skimpy foot-deep river flats, running, running, churning a white-water contrail. Epochal battles are fought from the stump pool, but mostly the canny fish win. They have an unerring sense for where barnacle-bearded, worm shredded pilings lay and where a last minute reprieve is to be found midst the old stump's long-dead root strands. But sometimes—gray mud on my forehead, cheeks and chin betells a beached fish. This is the stuff of dreams.

Chinook wakes wash to the heron's webbed talons. Surely a minnow will appear in the disturbance—a fledgling cutthroat or bullhead. But river-flow ebbs. Talons dry. There is no minnow. Not one. Clumsily, nature's ancient hoax lumbers aloft with a cantankerous "awuk" and is off downriver—round the bend, spirit in mist.

Chinook always hold a while in the stump pool. But not today! They streak through—blurred watery arrows. They come in singles and pods moving against the river's gentle out-flow. Bow-waves slosh and slop against a cross-river mud-bank and echo in late morning mist. Still there is hope. I cast and cast. But they are gone—gone up river.

Perhaps other fish will hold better down river—in that pool under the rotted pilings. Just where friend heron disappeared. You know the place, don't you?

The river's cycle repeats itself—over and over, year after year. Always the same and always different. And the fisher is forever hopeful.

My Stilly

WOODSMOKE RISES from a fire pit dug at the south foot of John Kruse's earth and granite dike on the Stillaguamish River North Fork just above Arlington. John's warm-up fire burns and smolders ceaselessly from the steelhead opener in December and on through winter. It is doused when the sprightly elfin farmer decides that the year's run has gone up river. Clad in black plaid wool cap and jac-coat, he is always on the move—casting eggs and lures from the dike's vantage points. Sometimes he sticks his rod butt in the sand and plunks, but even then he dances from one foot to the other. After our own forays along the bank's great granite rock cobbles in search of fish, we guests on his land gather around the fire to sip scalding black Norwegian gasoline and listen to John's tall tales.

No matter how big a fish we present for his inspection, the stubby, wondrously genial gnome has the story of a bigger one lost earlier in the morning or late yesterday afternoon or the day before or perhaps last year. "You know there's some great big 'uns out there. I seen 'um rolling just at dawn. You should-da' seen 'um. Make that one you got there look like a midget." His eyes twinkle. He is always optimistic.

"Say," he grins, "I hope you boys remembered to put your money in." He is joking about whether we have paid our quarter to his rusty tin Band-Aid box. It is nailed to a fence post at the entrance to the cow pasture where he allows us to park. "Sure did, Mr. Kruse. Wouldn't want you to be short on your next trip to the bank," we echo each other and cackle as our red noses drip and we shuffle booted feet at the fire's steaming embered edge.

3

"Bank, hell," John teases, "I still don't trust 'um. Anyway I'm saving up for one of them fancy poles like you guys got." But we know better. His rig is his good luck—not to be replaced unless some giant steelhead snatches it from its plunking perch while he is gabbing or prancing up the dike on an errand.

These days there are plenty of fish in the river. Lots of nice natives. We cast straight across the river from John's dike with #4 orange and white "Spin 'n Glos." Sometimes I move down river a couple of hundred yards to fish a shallow fifty foot drift where smaller fish hang out. Other times I cross the Haller Street Bridge and hike up river to fish opposite John and company.

There are problems with fishing this far side. The bank is overgrown with willows and tag alder, blackberry vines and other thick brush so there is no beach to fish from and very little room to cast. Because the bank drops sharply into four feet of water, wading is impossible—but oh how steelhead love to rest in this slow water—water no one can reach with a cast from the dike. How many times have I hooked big ones here and slid into the water over my hip boots trying to land them while John and crew shook with laughter, yelling raucous rebukes at me.

This is heaven! Not just because there are plenty of fish, but because there are always good-hearted souls around with whom to share hopes for a big one or misery over that monster that breaks off. There is a sense of comradeship among us even though we seldom see each other anywhere else. Somehow, the glue that creates and binds this atmosphere for me is the woodsmoke. Driving up the road from our house, only a hop-skip away, I look for the woodsmoke. Getting out of the pickup in John's barnyard, I turn my nose into the breeze like some human gun dog, sniffing for the woodsmoke. Casting an eye toward the dike's jagged ridge line, I anticipate the profile of a gamboling pixie, silhouetted against dawn, author of woodsmoke.

∾

Northwest Washington is my home now—the Stilly North Fork my constant companion. Some of its drifts have names— Monty, Elbow, Deer "Crick," Oso, Boulder, Hazel, Picnic Table, and angler-besieged Fortson. And, there are secret places— unmentioned except in whispers among "companions of the river." Occasionally, after a stirring sermon at Our Saviour's Lutheran Church about the Christian virtue of charity, a fellow worshipper confides to me in hushed tones over steaming coffee: "They's a pod of steelies up at Hazel." But secret drifts are not mentioned—not even in church; to disclose their location would probably be heresy! So I'm on my own and that's OK.

No riverbank is too steep for me to climb, no snowdrift too deep to slog through. When ice floes clog the lower river, then I fish above. Where ice edges lip the river bank, I skitter hooked fish up and over them. Freezing guides? Spray them with PAM. Keep moving, keep moving, keep warm. Tolerate that SOB of a game department guy who, during a pouring-down February sleet storm, makes me take off my waterproof parka to find fishing license and steelhead card in an inner pocket. What a horse's ass! Oh well, a cup of hot morning-old black coffee purchased at the Whitehorse store—with its logger spiked board floor—will chase away the evil spirits!

More and more I fish alone. I treasure the freedom to chase fish on the river's lonesome stretches. What of my Arlington friends? They know the good drifts and plunking holes—where the most fish hold, where the warm-up fires blaze, where there's company over cigarette smoke and a cup of pot-boiled Java. "Why the hell make a job of fishing, Paul? Hell, you work too hard at it." Perhaps I do. Still, the yen to explore leads me along less traveled paths to distant riffles—far from the woodsmoke.

My favorite water is above Hazel and below Fortson. To look upriver is to look into the snowy face of God—a mountain image framed in forest green. Closer by is the hundred foot fir snag where a great black-bodied and white-headed eagle peers into the river searching for overlooked bounty—maybe a salmon carcass.

The river here has few elbows—those deep water stream bends that are obvious steelhead holds. Mostly the flow is a grand expanse of transparent riffle. Anyone can see that there are no fish here. But that is not the case as I learn one bright February day.

The day is a beauty with brilliant sunshine shimmering on riffle water that is touched softly with green tint. By early afternoon I have walked forever—fishing a small pink bobber and yarn very carefully through a few elbow drifts. No luck at all. Trudging along a raised gravel beach that edges broad riffle water, I swipe a backhand cast out well across the river. Laboring along, a bit disappointed with the fishing, I am conscious of a great bow in my line as slack moves down river well ahead of the bottom bouncing lure. Who cares? No fish are in this kind of water anyway.

Then a jumping fish catches my eye. The fish is attached to my lure, but I feel nothing because of the line's bow. After landing and releasing a darkening hen, I get to wondering where the heck it could have been holding. There is only one spot that makes any sense. That is where a small boulder is sunk mid-river with a two foot deep pocket around it. But I can see into the pocket and cannot imagine how a fish could have held there. To get a sense of how the current moves around the boulder, I cast my corky to the pocket and am fast to a small buck!

These unanticipated events call for a "sit-me-down to think!" So I relax on a river-scoured log, light up my briar and consider what has just occurred. The riffle water seems transparent and

7

much of it is, but not all of it. There are nooks and crannies in the shallows that harbor shades of silver courage and make them all but invisible to the human eye. I have just witnessed a situation where I looked right at a fish and didn't see it. Perhaps there was a shadow that protected the fish. Come to think of it the shadows change with the sun's changing angles throughout the day. Perhaps the fish move from one pocket to another as the sun's angle and river shadows move.

Understanding dawns. I need lots of patience and a very keen eye to search each riffle for possible holds that are darkened by shadows. More than that I need the persistence to fish all the riffle pocket water. It is not water that I have spent much time on in the past and neither, apparently, has anyone else, for I hardly ever see anyone on the riffles. To think that the shallows are transparent is an illusion. That's the lesson!

Winter fishing with bait and bobber is good. But the North Fork is a "fly fishing water only" during much of the year— the period when summer steelhead swim. And herein lies the rub. How do I bring steelhead to the fly?

FLY WATER

Catching a summer run steelhead on a fly gets to be a challenge. Despite endless hours of casting, I cannot even get a pull. My good friend, Conrad Hjort, has showed me the canyon water below the log scaling station just above Arlington. He claims that summer fish hold in this run and are caught often by "the regulars."

Conrad is a kindly great bear who is loved in Arlington for his good deeds. He often tells the story on himself of the day when he was smoking a large catch of his neighbor's steelhead and was suddenly called into town to the Legion Club on urgent business. When he returned, the smokehouse was aflame and beyond help as were his neighbor's steelhead. Con likes to show off his new smokehouse, but no one brings fish for curing anymore. He keeps telling me that there are steelhead in the canyon water.

During fall the canyon provides lots of handsome sea run cutts. They hold in a dark, deep, slow run that undercuts an alder overgrown bank just above the canyon's landmark sunken car body. At dusk one September evening, as I am tossing Everett Bundt's Thor pattern into the run hoping for a big cutt, the fly is greeted by a hellish splash and yank. My little bamboo rod is bowed to the breaking point because I hang on tightly to the reel knob to keep the fish from escaping. I have never played a big fish on a fly rod! In desperation I release the reel knob, and it flails my knuckles raw—a blood lesson to remember!

Terror nearly overcomes me. Terror that I will break the rod. Terror that I will lose the fish. But finally, the great fish is subdued and beached. What a steelhead I think. Conk! Then, I remove the shredded fly and find that this is no steelhead, it's a Coho—illegal to take from these waters. What to do?

I wade back down river and across a wide shallow pool paved with spawning humpies and shimmering cutts. Up the canyon I climb, sometimes on all fours, through fir slips and scrub oak, scuttling over slippery brown pine needles. My heart is racing; perspiration born of fear stings my eyes and runs on my cheeks. Will that louse of a fisheries' guy be on top waiting?

I peer through the thick-waisted cedar and tag alder, stretching my scrawny neck to look over the canyon bank and into the weed overgrown parking area—ready to duck and slink back down the hillside. Is there anyone up there on top? Looks like not. I'm up there and out of there, hoping not to get arrested for some traffic infraction by Chief Gobin on the one mile drive home. Perspiration drips. Can I make it? Yes!

Walking into our house, I am careful to carry my fish on newspaper so as not to slime the rug. Mary Ann is there to

9

exclaim, "What a beautiful steelhead. Your first on a fly. Why didn't you blow the horn when you came into the carport? I would have come out to celebrate!" At dinner, Mary Ann wonders why our fish filets are so orange; she's never seen steelhead of this hue. I smile and continue on to other subjects.

For another two years I ply the waters with a cheap early-stage graphite fly rod; my beloved bamboo is stowed away—out of danger. Still, not a steelhead, not a strike. The big zero! Then one July morning a secretary stops by my office to tell me that she is taking fly tying lessons. The good lady drops a couple of black marabou flies with silver tinsel bodies on my desk and wishes me good luck. They're not bad looking flies. At this point I'd try a rag mop!

Friends at church on Sunday tell me there are lots of fish in the Fortson Hole and that they will take a fly. I, who have sworn never to sully myself by associating with the grunts who dredge Fortson, am desperate. What the heck, give it a try. Maybe I'll learn something.

So I arrive and begin casting the black marabou. A fellow on the opposite bank who can see the fly's drift yells that my fly is not getting down on the bottom. "Either fish it on the bottom or right on top. Steelhead don't like it in the middle. Don't cher know that?" No, I didn't know that. Better switch from a floater to a sink tip; the fish are hugging bottom.

Would you believe it? The gift fly and sink tip line work. Two fish on; one is landed and taken home—a bright hatchery hen. Next day, more good luck. The ice is broken and all that trite stuff! I continue to catch fish at Fortson when no one else can. I've found the secret fly! Except, the next summer no steelhead will touch it. But that's OK, life would be boring if I ever found the perfect fly.

Let me tell you about some of my very favorite North Fork steelhead fly fishing waters. They are compellingly beautiful and largely ignored riffles. Their flows are deceptive because they seem transparent with no fish evident. Holds within the flows are difficult to spot and tough to fish. The fish are spooky. The waters are remote—to be cast over in solitude and silence.

Fortson Water: A good trek upstream from the Fortson Hole takes me to runs and riffles where submerged as well as protruding boulders offer splendid hides for wary summer fish. I leave the well-beaten shoreline path and travel several hundred yards over cobbles and against the current, then through thickets of alder and blackberry bramble. My leader and fly catch and twist and tangle and snap in the brush. My patience is tried. In fact I hear myself say some bad words. Every time I come here, the same bad words! Apparently not many fishers make this trip. I have never seen another person here, although I have seen faint boot prints.

Creeping across deep sand beach and up behind the cover of a large boulder, I short-cast a well-weighted large Kaufmann Black Stone into the boulder's downstream shadow. The twenty foot cast no more than straightens when there is a ferocious grab and a big buck breaks water with a bulging slosh that splashes tidal waves from one bank to the other. Surely, he was holding in no more than two feet of water in the boulder's slight shadow. Big fish, short cast, shallow holding cranny— and a fly that probably no one else would use. Can life get any better!

Every morning at this time of year the sun's particular angle for two hours or so creates a triangular shadow against the opposite bank fifty feet below where the big buck met Mr. Stonefly this morning. I make another very short cast. The fly bounces hippity-hop like a chewy morsel along the shallow golden gravel bottom and disappears into the shadow to be met by a wrenching strike. But the fish is gone in a frothy flurry and so is Mr. Stone; I have held too tightly. This is nook and cranny fishing, filled with hope and the joy of surprise. Just one step above bait fishing, it is a solitary enterprise. I love it!

The morning is growing late as I tramp back to Fortson and beyond to the Picnic Table water. Perhaps the water will be open now. But no. A young guy, garbed in filthy cracked rubber yellow raincoat, soiled cowboy hat and failed black hip boots, is flogging the pool's head. A brown quart beer bottle protrudes from his raincoat pocket. The pool's middle water is held by a frail pipe smoking old rail of a man clad in tattered red and gray wool mackinaw and olive half-boots. I do not want to fish below him because he has first right to that water according to fly fishing etiquette. I sit on a rock to watch and wait my turn to start at the drift's head. But neither party moves and then the old duffer turns and removing pipe from jaw hollers at me. "Well we wuz here fust and we ain't leavin', so you can take your fancy-ass gear and go somewhere else." Such civility this morning!

Paul's Water: This is a very long, wide and apparently shallow run. Its bottom is typical Stilly golden gravel, but overlaid with boot-sized rock cobbles that make wading an adventure. Multitudes of larger rocks peek an inch to two feet above the river's surface from mid-river to the far bank. Channels and pockets are everywhere among the rubble rocks.

Almost no water in the run lends itself to the normal down and across cast used by many steelhead fly fishers. It is my impression that most people figure that there is no good holding water here, only good taking-a-bath water or losing your fly and tippet water. Then too, the descent into this canyon is long, precipitous and pine needled slippery. If you smoke much, forget about climbing back out! I have never seen

another fisherman here, except for my friend, Dean Geddes, to whom I introduced this water—named by me in my own honor!

To catch summer fish here I must probe every darkened pocket and channel. Mid-morning with the sun well up is the best time. My homemade black marabou leech with silver overwound marabou body works well; so does a similarly tied orange leech. My fly books are filled with patterns created from careful study of Trey Combs' wonderful, *Steelhead Fly Fishing and Flies.* Fly shops in Marysville, Everett, Bellingham and Seattle have contributed to my fly heap. I pester "experts" unmercifully about the "right" fly. Still, all I need here are my own two ties.

On this water I continue to learn a most important lesson about steelhead fly fishing: read the pocket water—find those nooks and crannies that provide rest, security and oxygen for summer fish. This run has scores of two and three foot deep holds; and, it takes at least a couple of hours to fish the riffle right. The fish are where they want to be and not necessarily where I want or expect them to be. But over time, I learn the shadow-water and holds. Short accurate casting to well-read water is the ticket. Use a wading stick and beware a dunking! I share a picture with you here—a picture that is forever in my mind—repainted from different days among different summers on Paul's Run.

Courage, a shimmering, slim, silver blade of fish, fans over yellowed gravel in the ebb-edge current and shadow created by a bleached white boulder that cuts the river-slick. Orange marabou dances tantalizingly before her nose and begins to rise as river flow moves it to shallows. At once Courage in a silver flash stabs the fly and is stunned momentarily by resistance from the hook set. She hangs horizontal and perfectly still in the current.

Courage, flexing silver arrow, pirouettes against a canvas of moss-shouldered rock riprap—a ballerina skipping on the river.

My Stilly

An enormous ivory bow in the fly line tries to catch her as she skates over lime foam and tip-toes midst rocky froth to freedom.

Frequently here, I have met an animal acquaintance—a big doe. Some years she brings a fawn. Whether alone or with her young one, she takes little notice of me. She is not spooky. Probably because this canyon's walls are sufficiently steep to discourage entry by most dogs and threatening humans. Although I always greet her with sweet talk, she ignores me and glides along about her business.

Paul's Run has never given me a steelhead early in the morning or even before ten. I should think fish would be less wary with the sun under the canyon wall and shadow all across the water. But not so for me. There's a mystery here.

Boulder River: The North Fork just above Boulder River offers a classic main drift with handsome tail water. This drift rests at the end of a fairly long forest path leading from the State maintained parking area. The water below and above the drift is a long broad riffle. Most fishers try their luck in the main drift and when done they leave or make a downstream hike to Boulder's mouth. Upstream a half mile or so is the car-body hole; but the hike is over slippery cobles that plague the wader.

I have fly fished the main drift scores of times and never taken a fish and never seen one taken, even though the water looks perfect. But that's not the whole story. The water just above and below the main drift is as intriguing as Paul's Water because there are so many crooked little rills within the river rocks where steelhead lay invisible to most fly fishers. This is the story.

The Stilly is up substantially this morning after three days of warm summer rain. Boulder River is kicking in plenty of color. I am a quarter mile upriver from Boulder and the color is fine. Just above the main drift's head, there is a six foot long and three foot deep cut of very rapidly flowing backwater. The water looks too fast to fish, but there must be protective rock cover on the cut's bottom for almost always a big fish can be found resting there. The secret is to get your fly on the bottom.

Sneaking across beach and gravel, I dapple a heavy nymph into the stream flow where the fly sinks quickly and bounces on gravel. The fly, leader and line stop for an instant and then zip upstream straight at me, three feet past me. Splash! Crash! Snap! Gone! The fish is gone. Should I be surprised? Not here. It happens just about every time I show up. The leader breaks or the hook pulls out and I talk to myself and even answer back. River drops are tears on my cheeks. Let's look downstream a bit.

There is a similar cut, no more than five feet long, a hundred yards below the main drift. It lays near a downed fir tree ball that has rested in the river for years. I caught my first winter run fish on a fly here—a fluorescent orange marabou leech that may remind fish of an egg. Fishing a fly through this funnel is like bottom-walking a worm. No cast needed, just dribble the bottom. But no one's home this morning—time to consider upstream water.

The upstream riffle whispers and twinkles in diamond highlights. Jade-green hills darken in the distance and meld with boundless forest hill country, top-edged with snow-field lace. Wispy mist-haloes brush the river valley from earth to heaven as if God has brought an especial blessing on this place.

My new destination is half a mile back upstream. The trip always drains me because slippery rock cobbles send me skidding and they bang my ankles while I push against the current. Heavy aluminum-cleated rubbers, worn over wading shoes, are fair protection from slipping, but they seem to gain weight every year. Experience and common sense tell me that the extra load is necessary. I 'spose some "sawbones" would add that all of this is good for the heart. Still, my heart is a-pounding and the sweat is a-drippin'.

I love to fish the long rod—the ten foot 7-weight. My black and silver leech plucks and picks here and there, but there is nothing for a quarter mile, perhaps more. Finally I am off the confounded cobbles and onto sand. But the sand is soft and deep and it is muckier than I had remembered. I retreat into the trees to struggle along a seldom-used overgrown path. Across river is a long, skinny, rotting fir snag laying exactly parallel to the bank over shallow water.

I have seen the snag before but never cast a line to it. "Why not?" I wonder. "Why have I never seen the bulge of deep green water just at the snag's upstream end as I see it now? Is it the sun's angle?" There is some kind of obstruction below the surface. Perhaps there is fish cover in the green.

My cast is intended to be sharply upstream and across so that the fly will have plenty of time to sink before it enters the green bulge at the snag's top end. But the cast is a flop. It lands right atop the green water. Nevertheless as the black leech touches surface film, a silver princess swirls on it. She is the river's medallion, huge, lithe and brave, no fin clips or hatchery-wearing on this silken wonder. She runs and jumps and jumps—a native dancer trapped in shallows.

I have to have her picture! That done, it's a simple wrist turn to free her from the barbless hook. Who would ever believe that such a fish could come from such a nook? Egad and on that most miserable of casts. You just never know—and perhaps that's part of what has always induced me to fish. It is what I call the certainty of uncertainty—the whole business of surprise. Oh well, time to head downstream now.

An older man and young woman are fishing close to where I lost the uphill swimmer earlier this morning. They are well turned out in Orvis duds, though I see no telltale labels. I sit and watch unwilling to interrupt their concentration, waiting my turn at the drift's head where the man casts a nice line.

He acknowledges me and waves me in to fish above him. "I appreciate your courtesy," he says. "My daughter is recently divorced and I am trying to help her take her mind off a bad situation, so I thought she might enjoy some time on the river. Maybe you're tired after all your wading. Try a sip of this." He pours a shot from a pewter flask into its jigger top. Brandy. I toast him and his daughter. She never turns in our direction. It's best, I think, to leave this water to them.

So I chug my truck up the Lake Cavanaugh logging road on a shortcut over the mountain to home in Conway—well-fortified with a huge paper cup of black morning-old Norwegian courage from the store at Whitehorse. It's that old place where loggers' calks have chewed history in the wood floor and the owner doesn't care if you walk in wearing your wading cleats. Along the way over the mountain road, I think again about civility.

Horse Pasture Water: Friend Dean Geddes and I meet this morning for breakfast at Weller's Chalet by the I-5 Arlington turn off. As usual it passes through my mind that he is trying to drive me mad. His breakfast is of enormous proportions and he lingers over every bite, talking to everyone who will respond and to others who won't. He is the world's most gregarious fly fisherman. Everyone loves him. He is a decorated Commander of the Acapulco Chapter of the American Veterans of Foreign Wars; he sends me pictures from Mexico to verify his office. He wants to talk and I want to fish.

We drive to our destination in his cumbrous, ancient, white travel-all. Its rusting exterior is covered completely with decals that proclaim hundreds of places he has visited. His little green boat hangs on slightly rusted aluminum pipes above the vehicle's roof, although I have never seen the boat in use. And inside the monster van—inside is Pandora's box—eight feet of green cabinets and shelving on each van side filled with fishing tackle, waders, boots, rain gear and clothes to meet every contingency. He even has a secret store of night crawlers—Dean's bit of blasphemy. I bet he has some salmon eggs in there, too, although he would never admit it to me.

This morning we park next to a horse pasture that abuts some very good water—one of Dean's favorite drifts. He dawdles over which waders to wear. "Will these be too warm? Do these have a hole?" Next comes inspection of the lunch his wife has prepared—as if he could do anything about it now. Ah, a nice red apple. He chats with the pasture's roan filly before feeding her his apple. I wonder to myself if his purpose in life is to keep me off the water. I cannot believe that a former world class stock car driver can be such a drag. "Am I slowing us down?" he grins. Dear heaven—at last to the river.

We are fishing shallow fast water today. That is because the river is so skinny. There has been no rain for weeks. I cast and cast to shadowed water against a steep bank overhung with alder; upon arrival this morning we saw a glint of silver there. Nothing. Rest the water. Whether in inspiration or exasperation I tie on a #8 Muskrat. Polly Rosborough thought it looked like trout food and sure enough it works. Perhaps steelhead smolts feed on such bugs and this fish remembered its infancy! Dean is impressed and begins pawing gnarled, machine-banged fingers through his fly boxes.

We move and are just below a short chute of very fast, deep green-blue water that breaks into a large foot-deep pool and a shallow run that travels along a riprap granite block bank. Surely there are no fish here in these transparent shallows. Ever hopeful, Dean tosses a #12 Hare's Ear into the chute and it is swept against the riprap and into slightly shadowed shallows. Tic, tic, the line moves slowly. We peer into the shallows. Nothing. Perhaps a small trout is pecking.

Two more casts with similar results, tic, tic. The next cast is greeted with a shower of silver. A big fresh hatchery hen runs Dean down the river. Perhaps, we think, there are times when ordinary drab trout flies that represent the prey smolts eat work better than our flossy counterfeits. Dean is not only converted, he is ecstatic. "Wait 'til I tell the guys up at H and H that we're catching steelhead on trout flies. Course they'll never believe it. Say, how come we couldn't see that fish laying there?"

Alas, the best of today is yet to come.

We always start and end the day at Weller's. Today we celebrate steelhead caught on trout flies. A new lady bartender is on duty. She is attractive, in her early thirties, and of brunette locks and olive complexion. Golden tongued and suave Dean is enchanted.

"Say, sweetie, ain' chu new here? I'd like a glass of white wine and anything else good you got to offer." He gives her that big innocent Dean smile. I'm ready to slip off my barstool and disappear among last night's sweepings and insect pests on the barroom floor. But the two new friends hit it off like a pair of ready-to-nest robins.

"So you guys been fishing," she says. "Oh yeah, we love fishing. How 'bout you? Do you fish?" Dean grins. She gives him a big wink. They talk and talk; smiles and smirks. It is getting time for us to go. Then the nice lady looks at my pal, that tall, handsome sixty year old cowboy and sparks, "Well, I live up on the South Fork and you can come cast your fly on my front lawn any time you want." As we leave the bar, Dean is chuckling to himself and I am hoping that this gal doesn't have a husband or boyfriend or brother around the corner waiting to kill the pair of us.

⌖

How I love this river. At Fortson, a drift shunned by many fly fishers because it is crowded, I honed my fly fishing skills and tested flies I had labored so hard to create. And laughed.

Laughed at the shady-acting character who insisted on fishing the drift from granite blocks on the drift's deep side—the wrong side—in an effort to snag a fish. Howled in delight as he hooked a fish and slipped off his perch into the drink with the snagged buck running for Arlington. Clapped my hands and hooted in glee when the doused miscreant scrambled to the beach below to be met by that lout of a state fisheries' agent. "Write him a ticket. Stick it to 'um. Fine him good," we shouted. Laughed at myself....

One fall day, fishing among several others at Fortson, I have a heavy strike. The fish swims on the bottom, round and round the pool. Others want to cast and begin to glare at me, "Pull 'um in for gorsake, pull 'um in." So I turn my back to the pool, put the fly rod over my right shoulder and begin to march up the beach to the woods dragging leviathan. I hope the fifteen pound leader won't break, but don't care because I am embarrassed to be hogging the pool. Soon, there is splashing and the goon who has been yelling at me to pull 'um in says, "Hey, watch out, you got a big dog; don't horse him; you'll lose him." A neighbor begins singing, "How Much Is That Doggy In the Window?" The leader snaps as my huge chum salmon's egg-laden belly drags on the shallow beach. Everyone commiserates—even though the fish is a dog! We sing of the dog and giggle.

On a summer day we are fishing the gin-clear water at Fortson and begin to hear a ruckus slightly upstream and deep in the woods. Thrashing, thumping, tumbling. The feeder creek at the drift's head turns cloudy and muddy and soon the whole river is too muddy to fish. Impossible! From the woods near the feeder's mouth a horse comes galloping out into the river. It is ridden by a barefoot young woman in jeans and T-shirt who swims her steed through the middle of our drift into the tail below and is gone in a splash down river. "What the hell was that?" someone wants to know. "A girl on a horse," answers a wag as we all depart for clear waters.

Beyond its fishing and lore is the Stilly's quiet. Its surround-
ings are soft. Once in a while the logging train comes chugging
through and the kids scream in delight as they swing off the
railroad trestle at Oso. Fortson can be a mob scene, though if
you are looking for entertainment or someone to talk to, that's
a good place to go. And then there are all of those other
places—the quiet places.

I look from the turquoise riffles of Paul's Water over my
river's golden cobbled gravel to upswept deep green cedar and
pine canyons to snowy Whitehorse and blue infinity. This is
my river. It is a place filled with the richness of uncertainty
and certainty—*where are the fish this morning? I know they are
here, but where?* It is a place of solitude and searching, invigora-
tion and enlightenment. It is a place to be alone where you are
never alone. There is poetry in this place.

Priest Point

To fish is to hope and my hope is realized this leaden early morning in late March. Pods of sea run cutthroat slosh and splash up the shallows. Moving on a gentle rising tide just a short cast away, they stir opaque waters, searching for shrimp, candlefish and small herring. I wonder, "Is there an alligator-sized Dolly Varden lurking nearby?" You just never know— you never do. Winter is gone and so are the days of waiting and fruitless trips to this beach. At last the fish have come. Another of nature's wondrous cycles repeats itself. Good show!

Priest Point, due west of Marysville, is a pine-studded highland overlooking the Snohomish River estuary a bit below Quilceda Creek. More than one hundred years ago, Father Chirouse, missionary Catholic priest and Indian Agent to the Tulalip Indians, lived in the great tall stone house on this bluff. That grand old monument is a sentinel guarding hallowed Indian ground and waters. Today, Dick Erickson, legendary Husky crew coach lives in it.

An eight foot tall gnarled stump is deep-anchored in grainy gray beach sand far below the house. Its stout limbs, polished slick by an eternity of wind and water-scour, are salt and sun-bleached gray-white. I wonder how it got here and if its past touched the life of that first cleric who walked this reservation. But the stump is silent.

Whenever I come to the beach, I look first toward the stump and then at where the tide is making its mark. How long to the high? Where is the wind? From the southwest and in my face, blowing bait toward the beach or from the east so that fishing is the least? These are a fly fisher's queries—not just for Priest Point but for all waters, for all times.

The best fishing is in early morning on an eight to ten foot tide and with only a little wind—two hours before the high to two hours after. Late afternoon and into evening on the rising tide is good too. It seems like the best fishing days are over-cast—high or low overcast. But then it's almost always overcast here in spring.

Fly fishers on this beach are gracious men—old school gentlemen. They are soft-spoken. One smokes his pipe with bowl turned down during drizzle, rain and occasional draughts of strong southwest wind. I've never before seen an upside-down pipe and marvel that hardly a pinch of tobacco falls out. Another weathered good soul draws on a pipe topped with silver wind-cap. The deep sweet aroma of his smoke mirrors the wisdom of his words.

> *You throw a fine long line, Paul, but you are probably unacquainted with the way we fish here. We cast three or four times from our position on the beach and then move down the beach three paces, make our casts again, and move again. That gives everyone a chance. Know what I mean?*
>
> *Say, Paul. If you want a chance at an alligator Dolly, come here before dawn and on the tide. Try this yellow and white marabou down there a hundred yards beyond the stump. See where I mean? Same thing with a rising tide in late afternoon. You just never know what might happen. But you only get one chance! That's all. I've walked out of here more than once, kicking myself for being asleep at the switch!*
>
> *Let's rest the water awhile now, Paul. Have a cup of Java with me and we'll just let the water rest a bit. Did I ever tell you about....*

The sages of this beach fish fine rods, gleaming bamboo with deep burgundy wraps, a slow sinking line and eight feet of leader attached to some secret fly. Each has his preference and I stand a lot better chance of knowing what Don Marquise is fishing than does Dr. Finley! I am new and young and the elders confer on me innocence—since despite their high regard for each other, there is always the edge of suspicion and polite competition among them. So I am the beneficiary of their shrouded shenanigans and advice. I learn important etiquette. Bless these generous men.

They tell of a six pound trout taken last week and they speculate on exactly what fly it was that Harry used last year to land a huge Dolly. "Course you know Harry, he's tied something that's an exact candlefish imitation. I know that guy. He wouldn't fool around with a herring fly. Course he wouldn't show it to anyone." And so it goes. Their hope is forever. Each one thinks to himself, "Maybe, just maybe I'll catch that big 'un. Maybe it will be my turn." But none utters the hope out loud, for somehow that would be unseemly among these anglers.

Mostly, I am alone here. My constant fly pattern is Al Knudson's Yellow Spider, purchased at the Marysville Hardware store. Whether cast upon the Stilly's North Fork or here, it is an extraordinary cutthroat fly. We parade up and down the beach together through slick and heavy water, intercepting fish headed for Quilceda Creek or the Snohomish. What a fly! If you use it, be sure that it has a little tail of red saddle hackle.

The cutthroat travel in pods that sometimes are plainly visible as fish dimple the surface in turns and flashes. I suppose that they are chasing bait fish or showing tail as they nose dive to grab shrimp. They are large fish, lingering in one place only long enough to clean up the chow and then moving on. Many are more than twenty inches long, the size of small steelhead, and they are plentiful. I never take more than one fish.

More often than not, the trout are present but do not show themselves. I suppose they are feeding on bottom critters. So, it is a matter of "blind casting" and hoping that sooner or later something good will happen. And when a fish strikes, I think,

"Well, I knew they were there. It was just a matter of staying with it. You can't give up." The lustrous Orvis Battenkill bamboo gifted me by my wife, Mary Ann, though we could not afford it, bows to a courageous fish.... Oh how I love this gloriously solitary place—a fly fisher's salt water paradise.

The tide is only a foot above dead low this late afternoon—creeping up the mud flats and stirred by blasts of south wind that churn it brown. Nothing is right for fishing, but I am on the water because my passion for the fishing and eternal hope give me no choice. I am here because I have to be here. "Maybe the big one will take. Maybe this will be a lucky day." Judging by the wind's velocity, odds aren't good. My best casts are only about thirty feet.

Skies darken, and horizontal rain sheets wash away the Everett paper mill smudge. That's a blessing. A black- tongued jack hits my spider and flips off the barbless hook. I tie on a big ugly yellow and white marabou streamer that imitates nothing in nature! Casting and moving, casting and moving; I am a hundred yards or so below the stump. Say what you will about waterproof parkas, the wind-blasted rain is soaking my shirtfront and my spirits are sinking. Drip, drip, the drops fall from my nose to chin and down my neck. My teeth are beginning to chatter.

No fish strike and none are to be seen—getting dark now, time to go home. I am roll casting and using long quick retrieves that end prematurely ten feet in front of me. Not a smart way to fish, but I am bored and frozen. As I lift the bamboo to roll my fly line into a forward loop, an enormous glowing copper spotted shape with jaws open broaches surface. Stupid! The fly is air-borne an instant too soon and "mister alligator" swirls head to tail and is gone. I cast again and again but the fish will not come back. All the way back to the little

Volks I scold myself aloud. "Damn it, that was exactly where Fred said a big Dolly might lay and at exactly the time of day he mentioned. And you're too dumb to fish out your casts, you dummy. Fish out your casts. Remember that next time, you klutz."

❧

I am the sole fisherman today until an hour before high tide. Four tough-looking grunges in hip boots show up, bearded, with greasy baseball hats, carrying a huge red-topped freezer chest and spinning gear. They will cast herring strips to waiting Dollies and they will certainly take some cutts.

The herring chuckers camp down beach from me a hundred yards and close to the front of a gray-weathered log house where a garrulous older lady lives. I have heard her fruity expletives screeched at dogs that dared trespass on her lawn and beach. She is not a creature I would cross.

The new arrivals have just cracked their first beer bottles when she appears at her front door. "I don't want you people cluttering up my beach with a bunch of trash. And don't take more than your limit of fish because I'm going to be watching you. And if you give me one word of sass, I'll have the deputy on you fast. Real fast. You hear me?"

Whether the guys are too surprised to respond or they don't have any time for her, I don't know. They go on chewing Copenhagen, swigging beer, baiting up, casting and proceeding to fill their chest with hapless fish. One gent is chewing and smoking a butt at the same time.

Just as promised a khaki-clad deputy appears with Mrs. Garrulous at his side, issuing instructions about how he is to conduct the arrest. The deputy confers with the scoundrels, scratches his head and walks off to his patrol car with the old woman shrieking at him. Seems that the beach is public, it has not been trashed—yet—and the fishers have not exceeded

their limit. The beery fishermen chortle and go about their butchery. On several other occasions I see these same men here, but never again do I hear shouts from the old woman. There will come a year when few if any fish are left to be caught here and the law will allow for none to be kept.

Although it is Sunday morning, my wife has excused me from church because the last good high tide for some time occurs today. My arrival is greeted by brilliant sunshine, and a little too much southwest wind. The gentlemen fly fishers are abeach in force, still in pursuit of the mate to a big cutt taken a week or so ago. Fly lines loop and my guess is that a lot of silent prayers are being uttered.

As I take my place in the casting line a head pops from the water no more than twenty feet from me. Big black eyes ogle me, while a shiny black nose sniffs and gray whiskers twitch with what appears to be curiosity. I am transfixed by the creature's stare, but I have no idea what I am seeing. The urge to flee is paramount. "What..?" is all that I can get out. Then with a silky smooth twist the harbor seal is gone and a fellow fly fisher hoots in laughter, "Just about wet your pants, din't cher? Don't worry, that's not the last one you'll see, but next time you'll be prepared," and he fires a cast into the wind.

By lunch time we have had our fishing and the tide has left us. As we are about to quit the beach, one of the fishermen says to another. "Too bad about Harry isn't it. I mean since he remarried."

"Yes," comes the response, "I haven't seen him on the beach since then and no one else has either. I hear she won't let him go fishing. By golly nowadays a guy has to be nearly as careful picking a wife as he does a new bamboo rod."

On the strength of that wisdom we go our separate ways, calling to each other that we'll meet again on the next good high tide. We are creatures of nature—willing captives of its cycle. As it repeats itself, so, too, do we—returning to this beach just as the trout return to these waters.

The old mission bell tolls noon at Saint Anne's Church above us on the highland. It reminds of promises to keep and promises to come.

The Samish

SALMON

OCTOBER—dawn edging slowly down the river. We are lined up—under, around and stretched out on both sides of the Farm To Market Road Bridge that spans thirty feet of Samish River; everyone is ready for that first cast. Whether the season will open is unknown. This is the scheduled opening date but a final decision has not been announced by fisheries' officials in Olympia. We await word.

"Here he comes," calls an eagle eye as the state fisheries' lieutenant's vehicle appears down the road. It is the well known blue Chevy with a spotlight at the driver's door side and a loudspeaker on the roof top. We stand poised for action. The loudspeaker booms, "These are closed waters. There will be no fishing until further notice." The blue car speeds off with "Whadda yuh means?" chasing it from voices up and down river.

Under the bridge, a bulky squash-faced young "red-neck" with the stolid qualities of a beer-guzzling troll and known among the local brothers as Ned growls, "Come under here and enforce it, bud." He goes to fishing. To trash the state fisheries' division is common practice here because its policies and practices never seem to be clear or consistent. Ned says, "Hell, they never tells you what the rules is, so you may as well go on and break 'um anyway." Good old Ned has paid more than five hundred dollars recently for out-of-season fishing and snagging, but that doesn't deter him this morning. Between casts he gulps great swallows from cans of malt liquor. His pal Carl, drinking an Olympia adds, "Can't those blamed bureaucrats see they's plenty of fish here? Hell, the tide is just right and

32

them elbow holes is loaded with fish. I'm fishin' anyway. If they write me a ticket, I'll tear 'ur up."

I'm not so brave. Best to head upriver where the cutthroat season is open. Prolonged recent rains lead me to hope that cutts and perhaps Coho or late Chinook will be in the river. The rules say I am not allowed to fish for or keep salmon, but if I catch some by accident and release them, what harm is done? That's the way I look at it!

Prowling the river road in my 4-wheel drive pickup, I notice another state fisheries' guy trailing me. He has a new car, but his skinny sneaky arrogant blond profile is easy to recognize. He has been in these parts for several years and no one, including his neighbors, has anything kind to say about him. Maybe we'll have some fun today.

I drive off the road across a slippery, clay-base cornfield to the river and an elbow bend drift. Parking bank-side and looking back, who should I see in the rear view mirror but "Sgt. Personality." Watching from the paved road, he probably thinks he's found a poacher! Will he take the bait?

I'm over the bank and wading a shallow tail to the river's other side where there's an overgrown cattle path leading up stream. Salmon fishing may not be open, but cutthroat are fair game and my gear is a 7-weight fly rod. Surely, no one could accuse this innocent of fishing in closed waters for large salmon with modest trout tackle.

There are no cutthroat. But late-run Chinook hit with gusto. Great fish lurk unseen in tannic elbow water. Some come to beach and some swim off down the Samish with my flies; the leader is only 3x—a little much for cutts and very little for Chinook. Except that Samish river Chinook are manageable fish because if you really pressure them after the initial hook set, and keep that pressure on, most seem to stay in the same pool where they are hooked. Not always, but too often to be coincidence. Two hours pass. Public Enemy #1 has

33

not appeared, but still, I've had my fun and perhaps the trap has been sprung. We shall see. Time to go. I need to get home to Conway Hill to split wet alder.

Climbing up the steep riverbank next to my truck, I pause to peer through a crown of grass hummocks. The fisheries' sergeant is lounging against the fender of his new Ford, glancing my way without seeing me but grinning slyly. "Gotcha," he thinks. "Another fat fine. Another few points toward promotion to Olympia."

"Well, hello Officer. Wonderful the weather cleared. Nice to be out here. I've got a thermos of hot tea in the pickup. Will you have a cup?" He is in a state of mild shock. No one has ever been glad to see him. Not even, according to rumor, his wife. Off balance what can he do but agree. "Where's your license and salmon card?" I supply the tea and paper.

He studies my fly rod and leader. "What'd you do with the fish?" he wants to know. "Sergeant, I don't fish for fish. I fish to fish." Now he looks at me as if I've been tippling *Grampaw Red Neck's White Lightning*—a potent brew made in the hills northeast of here. But he can detect no whiff though we are at very close quarters. With two counts of not guilty assessed me, Sergeant Unwelcome gives up and gives in to a bit of civilized conversation. Then.

He enters his vehicle and he proceeds to spin the tires. They slip and slide and cut down into the clay while the Ford's rear end sinks. Now he really revs the motor and his trusty steed soon rests on its body. Stuck. No way out. The trap has sprung. I am contrite and offer to go find him a tow truck. "No," he says glumly, "I'll just call in myself." My 4-wheeler pulls itself through slop to paved road where I park out of the sergeant's sight to await the tow truck's appearance. It had better be a 4-wheeler.

Sure enough Mr. Tow comes whistling by—all gleaming red and white, but not a 4-wheeler—oblivious to our sergeant's

34

flailing hand signals. Bad directions? Inattention on Mr. Tow's part? Who knows? Twenty minutes later Mr. Tow returns and without pause chugs across muddy slick to where my adversary beckons. Hook-up complete, the two men hop into their truck's cab. Wheels spin and whine. Mud flies—the gleam is off Mr. Tow. Now there are two vehicles mired a quarter mile from paved road. Time for me to go split that wood.

The lower Samish is affected by tidal flow for a mile or so east from the estuary up toward Chuckanut Drive. Today is perfect for fly fishing because there are fish in the river and there is a minus tide during daylight. On a minus tide fish are concentrated in dark three to four foot deep elbows and bends and against rotted pilings driven along steep banks years ago to prevent erosion. So off I go this early morning to the Farm To Market Road.

Walking down stream from the bridge is an adventure. Sage green tidal marshes above the riverbed are chest high with choking weed grasses and belly deep with tide-dug sink holes that appear and disappear. The river shore is heavy soft black muck that sucks like cooling molasses at my booted feet. It emits a sulfurous stink I have loved since childhood days on Cape Cod's Brewster Flats. I walk the shore edge with what feels like ten pounds of mud stuck to each foot. What a workout. Yet how lucky I am to have all this.

Pods and singletons of lunker Chinook and Coho flush from deep water hides and zip over the brown-yellow center river shallow flats seeking refuge up river. Salt is on the air and fish are in the river. How I love this marsh—sister to Padilla Bay. Just loafing here would be enough—to hear and see screeching gulls, barking geese and brant, nattering ducks and my old friend that taciturn ageless Great Blue Heron—in rain or salt mist or sunshine. And this morning I am especially lucky.

My bright red and silver fly reaches the far bank only thirty five or forty feet away, hugs bottom and occasionally a Coho takes and flings its silvered body along the surface in a shower of spray; sometimes a lunker Chinook hits and then broaches surface. When landed on the muck beach, a fish kicks up black streamlets that besmirch my face; frequently it chews ragged edges on my fingers as I remove the jaw-embedded fly. There are lots of fish but it is not easy to hook them on a fly; bait is better. Perhaps that is why there is seldom another fly caster on the river.

How many fish do I take? None. But my luck is exceptionally good, because there is no other human presence here down river. So my gift is solitude within a society of busy familiar creatures on a marsh etched as a timeless evolving masterpiece by eternal artisans—wind and water.

Many fishers are gathered in small convivial groups along steep banks below the Farm To Market Road Bridge this fall afternoon. The tide is almost dead low. Sitting over deep, almost still holes that they have claimed for their own, each group's members drift thumb-sized salmon egg globs on the bottom. For them, "plunkers" I call them, fishing together on a sunny day is a social event—with dogs, children and whole families welcome. Their tackle is stout—bait casting or spinning rods with sixty pound line. They use homemade landing nets with baskets four feet wide attached to extended hoe handles ten feet long. These nets are just right to reach down over the steep riverbank and to scoop up a thirty pound Chinook. The plunkers smoke their cigarettes and drink their coffee and beer and eat their sandwiches and talk and talk as they hope and wait patiently for the big one that will transform quiet into joyous bedlam.

Plunkers tend to be "up river people." They come from Skagit River towns—Sedro Woolley and Lyman, Hamilton and Concrete. Often they are referred to as "red necks." They are shaggy-bearded men who sport grimy baseball caps over unkempt heads of hair. Their plaid shirts and bib overalls are tattered and soiled beyond restoration. Their hands and fingers are stubby, powerful, dirt-crusted reminders of manual labor they perform—logging, farming, cattle or horse ranching, perhaps working in some half-baked auto and truck repair shop over on the road to Alger. They and their kin feel a claim to this place.

As usual they squint at me today with a suspicion that seems to say, "Hey, pretty boy with the fly rod, fishing vest, and neoprenes, stay away from us. We don't like your kind. Maybe you'll jus' fall in some sink hole and disappear." But they never speak and if I ask them whether they have had any luck, the answer is always about the same, "Not much."

I am wading the shallows a quarter mile down river from the last of the good plunking holes and have begun casting to a four foot deep drift along the steep far bank. Someone's mono-filament line runs from the opposite bank and into the deep drift—just where I want to cast. As I wonder what the line might be attached to, a thatch of blond hair under a faded cloth khaki military cap rears up out of the wheaten bunch grass. The hair has not been trimmed lately and this young guy reminds me of a talking grass hummock-head. He says, "Hey, mister, I don't mean to be a jerk, but you being in the water like that is gonna scare all the fish away. Then none of us is gonna catch any fish."

My reply is intemperate. "Hey boy, I fished this river this way for twenty years and I'm going to fish it the same way today. Maybe if you'd stop walking around and hanging over the bank, we'd see some fish." He is smoking mad but sinks back into the bunch grass. Just moments after "thatch top" has disappeared, a grand Chinook takes my fly and porpoises the surface sending gusher waves across the pool. The whole pool seems to rock and roll and tilt askew as the battle proceeds and then ends favorably for me.

"Thatch top" is impressed. "Gol, Mister. I'm never gonna argue with you again. Whatcha using for bait?" As he talks, he reels in his line. He is fishing with a dead, eight inch herring tied directly to a four or five ounce sinker and then to his line and back to the rod. I've often wondered who could have been so cruel as to suggest this rig to "thatch top". Whoever it was did a good service to "save the salmon."

The mile trudge back to my pickup is through chest high grass and around clutching brambles and blackberry vines—betwixt and between those confounded camouflaged sink holes. Afternoon has turned hot and I am sweating gum balls as I try to balance a big Coho and the bigger Chinook along with my fly rod. Loose grass seed is in my nose and eyes. It itches under my shirt collar and sticks to the sweat and mud on my face. My arms ache and fingers burn. Oh for another set of hands!

At last I am within sight of the road and am passing a group of "red necks." They take a good look, but say nothing to me. I hear one mutter to another, " Look at those fish. These bastards and their fancy fly gear catch all the fish and we don't have a chance. They ought to outlaw fly fishing on this section of the river."

STEELHEAD

Cutting frigid air pours into the Skagit Valley from Canada this December morning. Its icy bite is tempered slightly by warm salt mist drifting in from the bay. Where the two air masses meet, freezing ground fog is created and that's cold stuff! Nevertheless I slog along, boots crunching frost crystals that cling like white beards to dead brown corn stalks. Skim ice covers soft-bottomed mud puddles that flood the cornfield and run along its edges. Walking is slippery—the river a long way off.

A bald eagle, silhouette black, rides sky-waves high over the Skagit River. This magisterial noble is searching for Chinook or burnt-orange-red Coho that are dead or struggling in river shallows. To the east, just above the tree line near the Samish River hatchery, sea gulls shriek at an early breakfast of spawned out salmon. "Get fat, you scavengers. It's going to be a long winter."

The riverbank is a clutter of alder, bramble, and blackberry that prevents normal casting. Wading is impractical because brush overhang forces the wader into the deepest water—too deep to negotiate. I crawl toward the bank through a thicket of juvenile alder and get my face properly slapped; blackberry vines clutch my ancient gray twill wool jac-coat; thorns pick at my fingers. Only a damned fool would tolerate this torture. Few folks fish here.

The near bank is undercut by deep, dark swirling water. But fish hang throughout the pool—against the bank's tree-rooted clay ledge, at the pool's edges and even in its dark-water tail. The only practical way to fish this water is with a bait-casting rod stuck through the tree branches—bottom-bouncing an orange and white Spin 'n Glo decorated with salmon or steelhead eggs. I have named this place, "The Almost Impossible to Land a Fish Hole." There is another nearby down river drift I have named, "The Trees Are Too Close Together Hole."

Spin 'n Glo with its egg appetizer drops to bottom and swings underneath me. It stops where it should not and I jerk the rod sharply. Fish on! It is a little six or seven pound buck that surfaces once and beats along the bottom. "Typical plastic hatchery fish," I think. When it comes time to drag his dead weight up the bank, my leader snags a root and breaks. Fisherman's luck.

Tie a new leader; try a Sammy that is silver bodied with fluorescent lime-green yarn and add some eggs. At the pool's tail a pretty silver fish strikes hard and then swims back to me with thrashing but no vitality. Humph! Another hatchery fish. Maybe I can get this one. I toss the rod aside and grab the line. My right boot foot slips and slides into the cold water as I lunge for the fish. The leader breaks but I have the hen in both hands and toss her high up in the alders as the cold water tops my hip boot. If someone offered to pay me to do this I would tell him to take a walk.

Another of my favorite drifts is upstream. Its shallow, pointed beach is an ideal casting place. An ancient stump limb protrudes three quarters across the pool and over deep water, providing nice steelhead holding water. I have named this place, "The Damned Log Hole." One cast with my new Sammy and eggs elicits a strike and the usual outcome. A hatchery hen hops over the log and breaks off. No surprise. I sit and smoke my pipe and wonder why the fish in this drift always have so much more energy than those hooked thirty yards below. Well, one fish is better than none and so I slosh back to the pickup.

A change of boots and socks and pants and I'm ready to go check on the old timers who fish the old Route 99 bridge drift just below the salmon hatchery. The usual gang is gathered or I should say jammed in on both sides of the river. Several gorgeous steelhead rest on the shallow riverbank. Harry, of the stovepipe red hat, is furiously chewing at his cigar, spitting in the river and chattering faster than ever while playing a fish that is getting the better of him. Ed from Anacortes, puffing his Winston, has a fish that has managed to entangle two other lines. Everyone is laughing and having a blast except June.

June has fished here forever and lives just up the highway. This morning men on both sides of him have good fish and he has none. Old June is into a major pout because he cannot stand to have others catch fish while he doesn't. Seeing this situation, I greet him with a "hail fellow well met" and he glares at me in dead silence over his smoldering cigarette.

Neighboring fishers give me knowing grins; their eyes twinkle. They just love to rub it in to old June and get him to pouting. No matter how cold it is he never wears a hat and we all swear that when he gets into a good pout, his bald head steams in the winter-chill!

Great guys here. I have enjoyed almost twenty years of their back country wit and stories. Year after year each mans the same casting station—certain that his is best. They should install name plates on sunken posts here to hold their place from interlopers! As for me, well, with the crowd here, I'll trundle upstream to spend the waning afternoon in a little bit of heaven.

A short piece of fly water—that's all it is, but it has given me such joy over the years. A wide beach provides space to back cast, and the drift, itself, runs against a steep undercut bank held in place by stubs of scrub alder and fir. Someday the clay will come sloughing down and that will be the end of my "High Bank" drift. Few fishermen show up here because the hike-in is long and across a boggy pasture.

My fly this afternoon is silver-bodied with a wing of fluorescent green yarn. Believe it or not I have tied it to imitate the silver and green cork-bodied Sammy that I use so successfully in bait casting. Talk about a fly fishing sacrilege. Who ever heard of tying a fly to imitate a drift lure? Nevertheless, winter steelhead like the Sammy fly.

I release a gorgeous silver phantom—a native hen. River water brushes small stream-held boulders and with a whisper glides off onto golden gravel shallows and then around the bend. There is peace here and solitude and I am bathed in a satisfaction that is but faintly related to the fishing. This is a paradise of the soul.

Turning to watch my back cast, I see a young fellow walking straight for me from behind. He is a skinny guy—grime permanently impressed in the pores of a sick-looking gray wizened face, greasy black hair tied in a pony tail and bound with a thick rubber band. There is an aura of poverty about him and his clothes; he carries no fishing rod. "Can cher read the sign?" he growls. "No fishing is allowed here." To which I respond that I have fly fished and loved this place for twenty years and never done it any harm.

He is the new owner of a nearby down-at-the-heels shanty of a house. The pasture I have crossed goes with the house. This grinch has moved here with his family from rural King County. He tells me that he doesn't want fishermen walking his pasture and dropping hooks and gear that will hurt his horses. To my plea of innocence and suit for clemency, he mutters, "Ain't no uster askin' any more. I don't want no one roun' here." Turning away from him, nothing left to say, I plow through the bog pasture. My soul is benumbed by cold that is no creature of afternoon's dying sun.

Passing by the grinch's white shingle board shanty, I see two little girls—impish blondes with shaggy Dutch-boy haircuts. Clothed in tatters of filthy dresses that hike up to their hips, the children run and play midst wrecks of yellow and blue and red toys on the muddy front lawn. The little girls are barefoot in winter.

My beautiful little river is abundant with steelhead—sometimes. When? Well, one period seems predictable. That's near the end or just after a heavy snow fall. What is more, this weather condition seems to put fish on the bite. Maybe snow warms the water and brings fish up from the salt bay, while storm's end with a rising barometer triggers fish aggressiveness. At any rate...

Christmas is three days past; snow is on the bay. Crispy, dry flakes flood the frigid air. By three o'clock the afternoon is white-black dark and I lose my way, briefly, returning home from work. Six or seven inches of snow have fallen since noon. The view from our living room windows to Bellingham Bay only a short distance away is full-curtained by snow cascades. Tomorrow is Saturday. Maybe the Samish fish will cooperate.

My 4-wheeler plugs along just fine across the unplowed church parking lot. Wading in hip boots through a snow-drifted cornfield adjacent to the river is another story. I'm beat after a ten minute hike. No one else is on the river, there are no sounds, not even the screeches of gulls in the estuary or the whistles of hunting hawks. Snow stills the country this morning. I am the only visible spirit midst the serenity.

The steep riverbank is slick and I manage to slide down it on my backside, scooping plenty of snow into my boot tops. So I peel them down and pop out the dry snow, at least most of it; but more falls inward to melt around my toes. Oh well, you're not winter steelhead fishing if you're completely dry and comfortable.

Steelhead smack my little gold spinner on almost every cast. Fish are everywhere in the drift and they're on the bite. But there is a limit to how many times they'll hit a counterfeit. What a morning! I look cross river and see stark black leafless alder and willow limbs, skeletons of good times past, inked against an absolutely white snowscape. How perfectly exquisite. To have caught fish in such a place is a gift.

The way home is much slower going up Old Route 99 rather than traveling the freeway but I want to know if anyone is fishing by the bridge below the salmon hatchery. There is. A dog—a black Lab and brown something. Big chap with bristly wide face and alert brown-yellow eyes. He is a regular fisherman here who smiles a lot. Well-fed, he never pouts when he doesn't catch fish. He wags his big brush of a tail and grins knowingly when locals call to him: "Hello, Butch. Caught any today?"

Alone this morning, he is pawing in the slushy shallows. His prey is a very large and overage Coho hen. Paw and sniff and then a good snap at the Coho's tail and the process continues. After a while the Coho has had enough and sinks into dark water. Bristly Butch wags his tail, smiles at me and woofs, "My paws are getting cold. I'm going home. How about you?"

It isn't just the fishing is it?

Lore of the Dean

No Scotch! Two companions are pointing at me in dismay where we stand on scalding, sticky runway tarmac in front of Bella Coola's airport terminal. We are buried in luggage—bulging brown duffel bags and a neon-blue rolled tarp, a deflated red and black rubber raft, green metal boxes filled with groceries to last us ten days, fishing gear galore—but there is no Scotch—not one drop. Somehow, I have defaulted on the one responsibility assigned me for this trip to fly fish the Dean River's early summer run steelhead. I have forgotten to bring the Scotch. In embarrassment and shame I toddle through the terminal building. If there is Scotch in town I shall find it and have it at any cost. Such are the pangs of disgrace and despair.

My luck is good. A rusted-out once yellow Dodge taxi sits in shade by the terminal entrance. The driver's side is occupied by an Indian so large that his dark hulk fills completely the vehicle's window frame. For a pile of Canadian dollars he will take me to the liquor store. Agreement made, we barrel off spewing a wake of summer road dust and gravel.

"So where you headed," he wants to know and I tell him we are going to the Dean. "Well you better be damn' careful. Last week just over the hill here, a conservation officer got chewed up pretty bad by a grizzly. Took two rifles and two hand guns to kill that sucker. Them silver tips is in the low bushes looking for berries and they'll be on the river for salmon spawners. Stay to damn hell out in the open." Based on an exorbitant cab fare, this advice is expensive; so is the Scotch.

I know a bit about silver tips. In times long past, walking the trails near One Eye Lake and Nimpo, I saw their indelicate artwork—inch deep slashes high above my outstretched arms among great fir trunks. That was sufficient acquaintance for me. I became a true believer.

Riverman Tony Hill meets us with his flat bed at the lower Dean's gravel airstrip. We bounce through gut-busting potholes to just above the high brutal falls—falls that burst wondrous rainbow spumes where valiant steelhead and salmon climb. Only super fish make this trip. According to Tony, Smithsonian scientists claim Dean fish to be strongest of all the steelhead races. Thompson River enthusiasts argue otherwise.

Tony's narrow river runner rides strands and seams of gray-green channel as we bound upriver. When he slows to negotiate a bit of white treachery, broad ruddy brush strokes appear beneath us and are quickly swept away. Big fish—Chinook or steelhead.

We pitch camp on a sand and gravel bar fronted by classic steelhead fly water—a hundred yard drift from head to tail and just the right size for three of us to fish. Chores come first—dig a fire pit, install the cook stove and stretch a tarp over both so we can cook and stay dry in fog and rain; rig our sleeping tent and stow clothes and fishing gear well away from cooking fire; hang a clothes line. Last chore—hoist metal food boxes high above ground on strong outstretched tree limbs— no point in feeding bears.

Behind camp, tag alder and scrub pine growing in river-wash cream sand thicken and run up a heavily wooded precipitous incline. My compadres tell of an ice cave a few minutes uphill. They chip ice from it for the infamous Scotch and we sit on an ancient river-polished log blow-down. Orange twilight is spider-spun against purple sky. "Do you think there are fish in the drift tonight? There have to be fish here. After all we saw them below, didn't we? 'Spose one would take?" Scotch gives us Dutch courage. So...

Even though our licenses are not valid until the next morning, each of us sneaks half a dozen casts on forbidden waters. Poachers.

But we feel nothing and see nothing. Is it possible that there are no fish in the drift? Oh well, time for sleep, but no one will sleep this night. We are children waiting for the party to begin—wondering, hoping. Just as all fishermen wonder and hope.

Morning is a black eerie chill. I struggle with waders that must have shrunk two sizes over night; wrestle with boot laces that seem hopelessly snarled. My two-piece fly rod, stored carefully in its metal case so that no bear can make popcorn from its cork grip won't fit together properly; my leader tippet is buried in reel spool fly line. My fingers tremble uncontrollably as I try to turl Black Practitioner to tippet—trembling not from cold but from "buck fever." All the while, creation is flowing down our canyon—pale pink and yellow dawn touches us.

There is a hint of color in the river this morning. Good! Color gives steelhead a sense of security that brings them close along shore to rest among small boulders in eddies on beach drop-off edges. Ankle deep, I throw a little thirty foot cast up and cross stream. The Practitioner should bottom-drift just where beach breaks into deeper bouldered water. How many years have I spent over-casting close holding fish? How many sore arms have I nursed because I was too dumb to learn to read the water? My reading this morning is accurate.

On the turn my Practitioner stops and is wrenched away by a grand hen that porpoises down and across the river. Four times the great silver fish bulges on its way to the other side—and sails over the top of an overhanging alder branch where the leader snarls. "Snap" echoes on the river as fish and Practitioner disappear—all that fast. My hand never touched the reel handle. I never raised the rod. Never had time! Such was that steelhead's power and speed. "Did you ever see anything like it in your life?" is all the three of us can share.

Since the Practitioner is gone I try a Squamish Poacher—all glowing orange and tied on a gold hook. What a fly! Steelhead are bottom-hanging in a cut no more than twenty feet from river's edge and the Poacher comes to them on every cast. Their underwater takes are sudden violent yanks as if to shatter the rod or haul it from my grasp. Sprinting fish churn the surface and erupt in geysers mid-river and beyond—some tumbling over the rapids and then gone. Every one is into my backing before I can raise the rod's tip; the whirling reel knob is an untouchable blur. I have never been in such a place, never felt or seen such demons. Nothing in my life has prepared me to cope with all this ecstasy; indeed, nothing has even foreshadowed it—and I am reminded for just a moment of Thoreau's magical insight:

> *My life has been the poem I would have writ,*
> *But I could not both live and utter it.*

My companions, using shooting heads, seek to set new distance casting records; their flies sail forty feet beyond where the fish hold. By morning's end, the Poacher is worth about fifty bucks per copy, though I am not heartless enough to collect from my less well-provisioned companions.

All of the fish are fresh steelhead hens of 35 to 41 inches except for one huge Chinook buck that takes in the drift's tail, swims to its head and makes a general nuisance of itself by hanging on too long. The other guys finally shorten up on their casts and are into fish. For two days we have the drift to ourselves— except that when we wake in the morning, there are grizzly and wolf tracks around our tent.

Paradise is short lived. This morning Tony comes roaring up river with a band of three passengers who introduce themselves as a Chilean physician and two California developers. They have camped on this spot many times before and want to set up with us now. They have the whole river yet they want to be here; we give them no sympathy and no quarter. They are pleasant people but utterly thoughtless of peace and place on the river. After too much discussion, they establish a camp diagonally across river and upstream from us. We know that every morning they will row their rubber raft to our side to try to get into this drift ahead of us. So much for peace, quiet and civility.

Next day we are up before dawn and watch as the new arrivals assemble their gear and craft. They are halfway across the river in fast water when raucous clinking and clanking of pots and pans, cups and dishes sound from their camp. A black bear sow and her two cubs have arrived for breakfast. With hungry enthusiasm they shatter the fishers' makeshift wood table. Shreds of debris fill the air. So do shouts from the rafters who about-face. As they step ashore, hurling threats, the departing black sow looks over her shoulder at them with an expression that says, "What's wrong with you guys? We were here eons before you. This property belongs to us." The troops clean up scattered remnants of their camp and try to assure its future security. Alas they are late in joining us. In kindness born of belly-laughs we invite them into our fishing rotation.

As morning grows old I muse on hauntingly beautiful contradictions—fire and ice—a canyon blistering in July sun, yet close to an ice cave and overlooked by snow-crusted peaks everywhere on the skyline. A yell from our physician friend breaks the calm. He has a running fish, a big one. But there is a sharp "crack" and the man shouts to me, "Grab it, grab it." His fly line, attached to the fish but not to backing, whizzes past, enters the tail and disappears over the lip downstream. "Must have had a knot or twist in his backing," I think. "Wouldn't want to have that guy cutting and stitching on me." The six of us lunch together and discuss the day's action. There are plenty of fish.

Next morning I hear cussing from across the river. The fishers are hovering over their raft. After considerable study and discussion, one man launches the raft and rows like a maniac for our side. He greets us with two interesting tidbits. The bears, looking for a late evening snack, have found the campers' groceries to be delectable; through shortsightedness the groceries have been packed in cardboard boxes and not hung in trees; our neighbors will be plenty short of chow. Worse yet, they left some of yesterday's lunch overnight in their raft. Not too swift!

"You know what?" says the wet-seated rower of the boat.

"One of those devils bit a hole in the boat when he was cleaning up some lunch we left in it. Do you guys have a patch kit?" Sure we do and we share. "These bears should be recruited for some one's army," I laugh to myself. "Their guerrilla warfare tactics could take out a regiment of human irregulars!"

All is well. Our visitors are with us, having flown the river in their patched but still leaky vessel. The pods of hens to which we have been casting for the past several days have been replaced by big bucks. The water has cleared. The canyon is drenched in blazing heat.

For some inexplicable reason we are wading deeper and the deeper we wade the further out we push the fish. I have seen this happen so often on lakes and streams and other rivers—even on salt chuck beaches. And I wonder again, why do fishermen push away the treasures they pursue?

Afternoon's water has colored with snow melt. All is still—no fish moving. Heat has caused me to switch from neoprene to light-weight fabric waders. So, like some half-baked, two-legged horse, I am asleep on my feet, standing in two feet of water and casting when the shout comes. "Wow! Look at that beauty go." A Californian is fast to something big. Except that all is not well on the beach.

It is as if lightning has speared the man's reel. Parts spew from it like shooting stars shattering the river's surface. His spool is gnashing and gnawing its frame—screeching, grinding and then freezing. "Car-ack!" Under terrible stress from a large running fish, fly line backing jams and breaks in the reel's ruined frame. I turn aside and shudder great heaves of laughter. We gather round the afflicted soul. His reel has pieces missing and its frame is bent.

Spanking new and bought especially for this trip from one of America's great sporting firms, the reel must have become flawed during its production. But that is no balm for the shaken fisherman. He won't be using this reel again—not ever. Seeking solace, he reaches into his kit bag for a bottle of Canadian apricot cider. Marauding bears have left his cider untouched—at least temporarily. They haven't learned yet to remove bottle-top caps.

That evening, after our fellow fishers have returned to their camp, we find a star performer in slow-moving deep water just below "the bubble" near our drift's head. But we never identify the fish any better than to call it "Jaws." It strikes four times within twenty minutes and on each occasion it snaps or chews through fifteen pound test leader. We take turns casting to the prize, but we are failures. Then our fish strikes no more. Gone. We cast purple and black and orange. But with no response. By some marvelous caprice, the river brings us a puzzle—a mystery. What kind of fish was it? How big? Will we ever know? We cast and hope. Oh for just one more chance.

More broiler-hot sunshine this afternoon and my two companions are bored with the tedium of slowed fishing. They are captivated by thoughts of getting a close look at the grizzly that enters our camp each night. Armed with a sawed-off shotgun they head into the brush for a look. As their profiles flicker and fade among green-black shadows I think about the false self-assurance guns arouse in humans. So the afternoon ages and I change from waders and fishing to shorts and sipping a light Scotch and river water. I am a drowsy fisherman pleased to be alone and at peace in this promised land.

Yet, staring at a far-off mountain face that looks like a death's head, I am reminded of the danger implicit in this rugged fisherman's paradise. A few years ago a friend and I sat fogged-in for five days on a nearby lake; to have ventured our amphibian amidst surrounding jagged peaks would have been to court disaster. Another time, just three mountains away, that same friend and I in the same plane had found ourselves flying up a box canyon with forest fire smoke nearly blinding us. Unable to climb higher, we banked into a steep turn; the engine's high speed stall indicator sounded a klaxon that rattled the cabin and shook our very souls—on calamity's edge we gained safety.

Then there is this river. It is a bewitching turquoise jewel. Yet it is filled with traps. Some are obvious in white water, but others are invisible whimsies that wear soft disguises—disguises few humans can read. And there is the river's power—sometimes understated in slack water but never to be ignored by one who has seen unchained ferocity in those high falls—never wade too deep. All is not as it appears in this country. With all the delight it brings to our senses, still there is the shadow.

A jet boat engine growls from down river. Tony flashes by in a web of spray and waves his baseball cap in salute. He's headed upriver to deliver supplies. Returning, he stops for a quick chat. "Hey! The bear found your two genius pals. Chased 'um three miles down to just above the falls and they jumped in the river. He let 'um go and then tore hell out of the tires on a three-wheel all-terrain vehicle I parked there. They got the scare of their lives. 'Spose they learned anything?

Well, I'll bring 'um back if you want 'um." He is off with a laugh in gushing jet wash.

We're heading out this morning. Tony will be up shortly to ferry us back to catch the small plane for a quick trip over the hill to Bella Coola. Our friends from across the river have come over to bid us good-bye and to beg for our leftover groceries— onions, potatoes, rice, tea and some freeze-dried stuff. Nothing very exotic, but still better than what the bears left them. As they depart one of my pals of the previous day's bear hunt laughs, "Let them eat fish—if they're bright enough to catch one. Do you suppose we ought to leave those dummies alone up here? They might do themselves some real harm."

Our craft scuttles and scurries as it dog-tracks the river with Tony standing and steering from aft. Wise and wary he throttles up and down sensing our invisible course. That course is not straightforward. Everywhere there are granite ledges; many show as outcroppings, others as surface wisps, still others are hidden. Some are dull-shaped; they merely high-center a craft to capsize it. Others are keen-toothed hull-slashers; their kill is quick and certain. For those who misread the river or miss a cue, there is no forgiveness. The arrogant and innocent can expect no quarter. Even the humble and watchful can be certain that there is no certainty on this river. Still, fishermen return again and again to traverse these waters—all for the sake of hope.

Isla Holbox

T HE ISLAND shimmers—gray cloud-drift on an indistinct horizon—a journey forever away. It appears and disappears—more illusion than reality. Nevertheless our sun-blanched, twenty four foot sea-going fiber glass panga is swift transport across Laguna Yalahau from north Yucatan's hamlet, Chiquila, to our whale-shaped destination. We beach on white sand shallows and wade ashore to a thatch roofed palapa—home for two weeks. Sandflea, chief guide, and sole possessor of the island's commercial sports fishing rights grins, "You come just in time. Beeg feesh here now. Tomorrow we get them. We unload now. "

Young, handsome, whippet thin, short and sinewy tough, Sandflea laughs and jokes as we debark. But he is grave and almost stern when he speaks of tarpon. His tone and eyes become steel serious. Here is a man of intelligence and purpose. He will take us to the fish. I know it in my bones. Whether I can make the cast, jump a fish and even land it—that's up to me.

Our huge palapa's thatch dome admits sunslants to illuminate a great room where empty beer and booze bottles clutter every tabletop and counter. Maroon-painted cement floors are splattered with dried white beach sand and littered with leader snippets, purple and black hackle feathers and dried cockroach shells. No one has swept this joint in recent history. But the small rusty white fridge bulges with countless bottles of dark Superior and light Sol cerveza. Duffel and rod cases stashed in our bedrooms, we gather to receive Sandflea's instructions.

He examines my tarpon flies with disdain. I've spent plenty up north to be sure I bought or tied useful flies. "Very good," intones Sandflea. "Good for nothing! Your hook is too small. You need a 4/0 like this." He hands me a three inch purple and black fly—a horror that imitates nothing known to man or fish. And he laughs. He fingers my lovingly built tarpon leader—Bimini twist and triple Huffnagle with twenty pound class section and eighty pound shock tippet. "No good. You need twenty five or thirty pound test class section and one hundred pound test shock tippet. Retie."

He describes shattered tackle disasters of last week's fishermen who insisted on using less than gargantuan materials. One successful fellow, using the big stuff, was towed six miles to Chiquila before he landed and released a fish estimated at 180 pounds. "OK Sandflea, you win!" The cerveza is disappearing fast now as we become increasingly jumpy. A hundred pound fish! I think, "Dear God, what would I do with a hundred pound fish on a fly rod?"

Up before dawn we greet Sandflea who arrives with steaming black coffee and *pan dulce* prepared by his wife. Good stuff, but we're in a hurry to be on the water. Two eighteen foot pangas are pulled up in cool shallows; Sandflea will pilot "Mr. Sandflea" and brother Darwin will operate "Mr. Tarpon."

After ten minutes at high speed we are on the fishing grounds. Sandflea and my friend Bill, a professional guide on vacation, peer intently across miles of flat fifteen foot deep water. They insist that I take first turn on the bow. *Nothing yet. Nothing yet. Waiting. Forever waiting.* Forty minutes pass. I am so tense I feel like I could break. I've never cast a twelve-weight fly rod except to practice—let alone cast to a tarpon. If I miss my cast and slap the back of my head with this 300 grain Teeny line, I'll be in the drink—with a headache to boot!

"They come now," says Sandflea. He is so matter of fact. I cannot see the fish. Then I do. A two hundred yard wide churning wave moves fast toward us. White mist glows and shimmers above the wave as dark backs and dorsals crease surface. My stomach boils and bubbles and I am on the verge of shaking. Sandflea is poling like crazy to get us within casting range as the fish pass. "Cast now, Pablo. Cast now." I do and fluff the cast. Not far enough. Damn it. Not far enough.

Fiddling with excess uncast line, I see a great burnished silver ghost turning two feet below the surface and twenty feet in front of me. "Streep, Pablo. Quick! Streep Pablo." And I do and the grand fish is on and into the air—more than six feet of shimmering silver jumping higher than I stand. White spume blasts against blue sky. "Set the hook some more, Pablo. Do it again." And I do—with hard strip sets. The fish bounds off fifty feet and jumps in white froth geysers. "Bow to the jump, Pablo. Bow!" And I do. The fish is on the reel. Now I feel good. I'm doing things right. No jelly-belly, no shakes. Win or lose I win! To have had the giant on is enough. Meantime, Sandflea has his arms wrapped firmly round my waist. He's afraid that *el sabalo grande* will steal me away! God, how I love all of this. I am so lucky!

I pump and reel, pump and reel. But the end game is long. Too long. It goes on and on. An iridescent silver slab hangs thirty feet out from the boat and gains leverage from a slow running tide. With rod tip low I haul and pull, but to little avail. Friend Bill cautions, "Don't hold the rod that way. You'll break it." To which I growl and laugh at the same time, "Mind your business. I've caught plenty of big salmon." But not this big—not by a long shot! Soaked in sweat, I am chugging Sol, stumbling with the sea swells, holding on—pumping, pumping.

Sandflea and Bill have the fish and draw her over the gunwale for pictures—while the fish deposits quarts, maybe gallons of brown-gray crap all over the boat but with special attention to valiant Sandflea. Her mouth could capture my head; her eyes are unworldly ebony half dollars. Such a heavy

g. Ellis

beast. Sandflea and I struggle to hold her up for pictures. Then Silver Queen is in the water and recovering, held lovingly by jubilant, victorious Sandflea. Strength restored she glides down and away—silver specter blending into green blue.

"Lucky Pablo! Lucky Pablo!" enthuses Sandflea. "You know how long it takes some people to catch a tarpon? A year maybe two of steady fishing. I know that. You are a lucky man, Pablo. Most people never catch a *sabalo grande* like theese. Lucky Pablo." Bill is wild-eyed with excitement. He wanted this fish for me as if it were his own.

Bill jumps the only other large fish of the morning. With one false cast, he lays eighty feet of line straight to the head of a crossing pod. A mammoth fish bursts skyward. To the end of my days, I will remember Bill, leaning into that fish with his arm fully extended in the classic bow. Then an eruption and "twang!" Black-purple fly and orange fly line zip back and collapse in a heap at boat side; Bill slumps, head bowed in disappointment. Angler's hope; angler's luck. Not this time, mate!

By mid-morning the wind sets up a chop and the bay is a potato patch. With such wind, it is impossible to see and track fish. Time for a trip to the mangroves for baby tarpon—to Sandflea's "secret place"—a twenty foot wide shallow, clear creek. Armed now with 8-weights, we look upstream from the creek mouth to see a dozen fish swimming toward us. They are five-pounders. Sandflea claims that no one else has ever fished here.

Bill and Sandflea want to show me a good time and so I am first on the bow. "Cast Pablo. Cast." And I do—five feet short. "Cast again, Pablo." I do not cast again, nor do I retrieve the fly, nor do I speak. The fish keep coming and just as they reach my bottomed-out fly, I begin to strip it fast. A tarpon is on it and in the air, stretching up into overhanging mangrove brush and then down, "splat" and up again. Success—my first baby tarpon. We return it quickly to join classmates that have scattered upstream and regrouped. Back they come.

Bill, on the bow now, makes an incredibly long and elegant false cast and then snags his back cast in a bush. He is saying bad words as I lay out yet one more fluffed short cast to jump and land another fish. But then the master gets with it and stays out of the brush for a while. Our excitement continues despite an occasional bushy back cast. Tarpon are all over our flies. Neither the baking heat nor humidity quells our enthusiasm.

Racing home over back-busting shallows' chop we hoist cerveza toasts. What a blast! And I think to myself, "This is the place where dreams become reality."

Standing under drippy tepid water in our grungy shower, I ponder why big tarpon look brownish to me when they are underwater and at a distance. My thoughts are interrupted by, "Aye, ya yi ya yi!" repeated several times in an hysteric male soprano that resounds throughout the palapa. Three of us and the singer rush to the great room. "Damn it! He got me! A scorpion! I saw it. Stepped on it. Damned thing hooked his stinger up over my flip-flop and stung my little toe."

The queries fly. "Did you kill it? Does the sting hurt? Is it swelling? Did you bring some medicine?" Alas, our wounded physician friend is in dire straits. For he announces, "It's swelling and I didn't bring anything for scorpion stings—just diarrhea stuff." He is into the fridge freezer where a bottle of Beefeaters gin sits next to a bottle of Tanqueray. I didn't know a swig of gin was good for scorpion stings. "What a courageous guy," I think.

But no. Not a drink, not even a sip. Instead he lays the bottle of viscous Beefeaters over his toe. We three are so nervous that we each dive into the fridge for cerveza and watch expectantly for swelling or death or something equally terrifying. None of us ventures forth to our mate's room for an encounter with the scorpion. After half an hour nothing astounding happens. *Suffering toe* turns brilliant red but swells only a little. Our venturesome friend returns to his room, finds his helpless nemesis writhing on its back, administers a vengeful *coup de grace* and deposits crushed remains in the scummy toilet bowl. So much for intruders. *Stung toe* recovers sufficiently so that we all set off for dinner.

It is a five minute walk from our palapa to the town square. The street is hard-packed beach sand edged by modest houses and shops of aging alabaster, cement blocks or tin and thatch. Loaded clotheslines drape back yards. Shops offer fresh chicken or vegetables and sundries like pure water and popsicles. There is the local commercial fishermen's meeting hall, yellow-walled Posada Ingrid, the public phone and fax office. Adults sit on their door stoops and chat, children bat balls, dogs lay half buried in sand holes they've dug to keep cool; an enormous pink, bristly pig slinks by, trailing a tether that bespeaks only temporary freedom. There is a pleasant tranquillity here or so it seems.

We are about to ascend the rickety wooden stairs of an open air second story restaurant when Sandflea orders a halt. He introduces us to a striking, slim young woman who has appeared from nowhere. Sandflea calls her the Chocolate Lady or La Chocolaté. Dressed in tight red halter top and blue cut-offs, she is a Jamaican vacationer whose complexion is like glossy rich light chocolate. Her smile, set off by brilliant crimson lipstick and dangling gold hoop earrings, sparkles and glows in the twilight. She studies us a moment, giggles and is gone—a spirit. Sandflea says that she visits the island frequently. Sometimes, late at night, according to Sandflea, she walks the lonely beach, singing softly and strumming a mandolin.

Dinner generally begins with a huge platter of seviche—a mixture of raw fish, shrimp and lobster marinated in a blend of lime juice and spices and served with crisp tortilla chips and Sol. Often, the main course is a giant cheese pizza topped with lobster and shrimp, or there is fresh snapper or snook served with cheese breads. But tonight we lust for lobster.

That's a problem. Lobster will not be in season for several days. Sandflea and the waiter converse in muted voices, each casting furtive looks into the town square. Sandflea reports to us that despite the lobster season closure, the restaurant has them. Unfortunately, the fish warden is in town. Nevertheless, the decision is made that lobster will be served. Eight PM now, church bells call, and faithful elderly ladies, *Las Señoras*, are gathering at *La Iglesia Catolica*, kitty-corner across from us; few *Señores* are to be seen. Char-broiling lobster scent fills the air and drifts out onto the plaza. Bet folks below can smell this lip-smacking stuff!

Sharp-eyed Sandflea's mouth is agape. He has spotted the fish warden walking past the Catholic Church. Surely he will not come upstairs to the restaurant. Wrong! In short order he is conferring with the waiter who refers him to Sandflea. Earnest and prolonged conversation ensues. "Do you think old Sandflea will get arrested?" I chuckle to Bill. At last the lawman leaves and Sandflea returns to his seat. He does not report anything to us and we never learn the discussion's outcome. At least no one goes to jail!

As we finish dinner the village square fills with adults and children. Little girls are dressed in neat, clean, brightly colored shirts or ruffled blouses and skirts or shorts. The boys started off from home similarly neat but are play-tousled and wild with jet-black hair flying. Many amidst the crowd play foosball at a dozen tables and we join in for a little while. Drinks and snacks are served from booths just opened. Everyone is enjoying the warm June evening. All is well.

Thunder and lightning storms pester us all afternoon. But the weather change is reprieve from cloying heat that has boiled us.

After sheltering briefly on an islet from a passing deluge we are back out to fish. Lightning-streaks crease the southern heavens, and thunder rumbles over us. The oily sea is flat and reflects an ominous leaden sky. This is not a good place to be especially with a graphite fly rod in hand. I know better.

Still, we stand there, Bill and I with our rods hanging down into the water—supposedly we are grounded. Bill is dragging twenty feet of Teeny 300 sink tip line and philosophizing with Sandflea. Irv and Jim, fishing with Darwin, both have fish on—Jim loses a large barracuda that quickly slashes a hundred pound shock tippet and Irv lands a mid-sized tarpon. Without warning, Bill's rod yanks down into the water. As I tell him he has bottom, the trip's largest-yet tarpon bursts sky-high at boat side. I am completely stunned and shout across to our friends, "Hell, he didn't even cast. Can you beat that?"

This is Bill's biggest fish of our trip and he wants it so bad that he is praying out loud. Either his prayers are answered or he is as lucky as "lucky Pablo". For as the fish runs out sixty feet we see a great knot-caused loop in the orange running line. Out goes the loop without snagging a guide. Then the fish swims to us with Sandflea guiding knot and loop through rod-guides as Bill reels in. Like a tame creature, the tarpon holds twenty feet out from the boat for the minutes it takes Sandflea to untie the knot. Prayers continue and then Sandflea has finished. Now the fish runs and jumps and acts normal! After the long end-game, she is boated, measured, photographed and released—a prize. Lucky Bill. But I cannot let my friend off the hook.

"How can you say you caught that fish legitimately when you never even cast? That's not fly fishing. That's jigging." To which he grins. "It's legitimate all right. I caught that fish from the pre-cast set. That's the same as fly casting. It's just that I was getting ready to cast." Later that afternoon we three friends of his, sipping cervezas, critique his technique and logic and howl in laughter. Our leader is no better than a jigger! Irv offers to make a "for sale" instructional video of Bill standing motionless for twenty minutes in his pre-cast set. This will be a best seller at home in Bill's *Blue Dun Fly Shop*!

But there is more to this "technique" than is immediately apparent. Several big tarpon are caught in our party by accident as folks inattentively let twenty feet or so of slack line drag close to bottom. What's going on? The answer seems quite simple.

There are large numbers of fish here and the majority of them, including many of the big ones, feed close to bottom. Their visual range in this clear fifteen foot deep water is good. When a fly is constantly drifted and fluttered just off bottom, chances are excellent that a fish will see and perhaps take it. How many trout have I caught bottom-drifting a leech from my float tube? The lesson: keep your fly in the water!

Conversely, fish seen and cast to on the surface represent only a fraction of those available—so the fisher is seeing a relatively small number of fish and making a limited number of casts. This hunt and fish technique usually means that out of every hour, fifty minutes are spent searching for surface fish; five minutes positioning the boat for a cast and then only a couple of minutes for a cast or two. Don't get me wrong! There is nothing like sight-casting to a specific fish and having the fish take. Still....

In either case the guide must take into account the wind and he must know currents and fish lanes at various tides. When sight fishing he must see fish at some distance and then, taking wind, current and tide into consideration, place the boat on a course to intercept the fish. At the last moment he must pole strongly to position the bow so that the right cast can be made at the right time to the right fish. And—the guide must keep his pole down so that back casts don't get wrapped around it! Nothing less will do. Timing is everything. Sounds easy, but it ain't. Sandflea is a master guide—smart and strong.

Los Viejos, the old men who know, say that there will be much wind today and so I decide not to fish. There is more to fishing than the fishing and the "old men's" prophecy gives me good reason to stay ashore. As my companions prepare to leave for the day, Bill says that the guides wonder if I am upset with them. "You know better, Bill. Tell them that no matter where I go on an extended trip, I never fish every day. Fishing is too important to go every day."

Today is a day for exploring the town and beach. In town I find morning Mass in *La Iglesia Catolica* is to begin. For a moment I contemplate entering church and then decide to participate from the park bench outside. Hymns and liturgy—all so familiar even though they are in Spanish; remembrance of early childhood in my grandmother's Saint Mary's Polish Catholic Church where Father Missa spoke a language I could feel but not understand; remembrance of childhood in my parents' Saint Margaret's cathedral where nuns tried with limited success to get my pals and me to memorize the Baltimore Catechism. So much for spiritual nourishment. I'm off to breakfast.

The town drunk, a skinny guy carrying a perspiring brown glass quart of beer, staggers me a "Good Morning Sir" in unaccented English and is off down the street dodging another escaped porker. A tiny four table restaurant feeds me delicious fresh-squeezed orange juice, a banana and melon frappe, followed by scrambled eggs with shredded ham and black beans on thin, tender, crisp tortilla chips. The nice waitress tells me, " *Señor. Los huevos y langosta. Otra vez, Señor.* " Right on! "*Verdad!*" If heaven is anything like this....

67

I am several miles up beach from the palapa, walking powdery white sands, when six black forms appear on the horizon. They move back and forth from beach shelf to mangrove edge. Are they priests? Nope—Mexican army troops, adolescents sporting adult mustaches and scowls, black-clad with black machine pistols and accompanied by three flea bitten mutts— an ominous array of talent.

According to restaurant talk here, Isla Holbox is a transshipment center for cocaine. Planes drop the drug and it is taken away by boat. The army maintains a permanent troop force here to patrol the beach. I happen to know that today, these blokes are looking for ten pounds of "coke" still unrecovered from a recent hundred pound drop.

The black suits study me, frowning deeply, as if I may have booty concealed in my swim suit! After questioning, I am dismissed. It occurs to me that the Mexican government might dress its troops in more suitable gear: maybe cool, tropical camouflage uniforms, rather than the easily seen dead-black hot fatigues. But who knows why governments do what they do. Still, being stopped by these sinister-looking chaps causes me to realize that there is a dark side to Holbox. All is not as it seems.

Returning with my story to the palapa, I find that Bill has broken another rod. Some luckless baby mangrove tarpon of twenty five pounds got involved with a Sage 8-weight manhandled by our leader. The rod lost—busted off at the handle. We chide Bill for his proficiency at destroying good tackle— admonishing him to be a better teacher. He grins that he is teaching us how not to break rods.

Days march on. So does the bug attack on my repellent-sprayed legs. Night bites have continued regardless of anti-bug juice applications and my legs are covered with yellow splotches encircled in sick gray rings. I am worried because neither prolonged immersion in salt water nor packing with wet baking soda heals the sores. This calls for drastic action.

So I learn to sleep in a nylon mesh hammock hung above the bed of torture. In a fit of pique, I spray a deadly pesticide brew over the sheet and mattress on which I have been sleeping. Later examination of the killing field shows hundreds of black pin-head sized mites DOA! After three days of not sleeping with the mites, my sores heal. The hammock has another advantage. It is not easily accessible to scorpions. Saddam Hussein has nothing on me when it comes to chemical warfare.

Fishing on the big water is good if the wind is down. We see fish and jump plenty—catching the few we deserve. When the wind is up we run to the mangroves and try for baby tarpon. For me this is very difficult fishing because deadly accuracy in casting is required despite very gusty winds. And we never do discover a killer fly for baby tarpon or snook. For me mangrove fishing is a lesson in humility.

Sometimes after fishing the big water until late in the morning we lunch at wonderfully special Ojo de Agua. Located on the mainland a few miles to the east of where we fish, there are two fresh water springs. They rest a hundred yards up a narrow but navigable stream from the sea. Their edges are darkened by gray siltish sand and so they resemble eyes. The springs create a fifty foot long, twenty foot wide, seven foot deep pool, shaded by lush jungle. Before lunch we jump from boatside for a refreshing swim in clear, cool, bubbling water. Eating delicious, thick chicken sandwiches that Sandflea teases are made from shredded Iguana, we watch parrots flitting high above among their hollowed out tree nests.

Wondrous occurrences highlight our Holbox days. Bill hooks a giant fish, breaks his rod at the second ferrule and ends up hand-lining his quarry into the boat. I hook a fifty-pounder that literally begins flight over Jim who is standing on the bow casting platform; with a mighty pull I haul the fish off its jump and into the water before it can knock Jim overboard. Then the fish swims off fifty feet, jumps again and sling-shots back the fly which ends up impaled in my knee; no harm done because the hook is barbless. Sandflea insists on trying to catch a crocodile with a fly. Another day, one of our group jumps a good tarpon right into the boat midst rods and a scrambling Sandflea who flies up on the outboard motor to avoid the mayhem. This is reality!

Gusty winds blow slate-green sea chop from horizon to shore this morning. Looks rough out there. No matter. We're not fishing today. We're packing and I'm studying every garment and bit of fishing gear to make sure no scorpions, cockroaches or similar critters are hitching a ride. Guess I shouldn't be too worried about their survival. When I get home, my wife will transfer all clothes immediately to the washing machine; and me to the shower! I'll scrub until my brown skin bleaches like the sparse white feathers that cover my pate. No bugs on me!

For months I dreamed of this island—knowing little of it because little has been written. I have imagined and wondered and above all hoped—hoped for something I could not imagine. And what did I find? Fish—leviathans with courage and strength beyond imagining. Towns folk—of congeniality and sublime cookery; the town drunk, our ever-thirsty early morning companion of the brown bottle; that ever-illusive, La Chocolaté—the Chocolate Lady who Bill claims has serenaded him late at night on the beach; and friend Sandflea—hunter and friend of the tarpon. The town—of cluttered, becolored stucco shops and houses along sand streets that lead to a red and yellow beflowered square that echoes with the tolling church bell. The island, itself—engulfed in fertile sea with

powdered beaches, pink-orange flamingoes, and endless man-grove swamps. I could never have hoped for all of this because I could never have imagined it!

As we prepare to board the panga for Chiquila, the beach is bereft of its fishing fleet. Commercial lobstering opened again this morning, so most pangas are on the twisting, churning gulf waters. The beach is deserted—but that is illusion for the fleet will return shortly, laden with lobsters and boisterous, thirsty fishermen. Our sea-going panga turns into the wind. "So long friend Sandflea. So long. See you next year." He stands expressionless, absolutely alone and still and disappears in the island's gray haze-smudge.

Joy at Christmas

FISHING WITH THE MAJOR

OUR Air Marshall Islands DC-8 creeps over early morning's last ghostly cloud flimsies. We are creatures of the night arriving at dawn. White-bodied with blue and orange trim, the dinosaur-jet crosses pale yellow coral beaches, muted lemon green lagoons and drab sage coconut groves anchored in buff sands. All this earth-color will be transformed to radiance at sun's full touch. Beyond the atoll's reef and surf line is first light's purple-black ocean. The Captain intones:

> *Just to let you know, folks. We're here and we're going to make a quick pass over Cassady's runway to make sure there aren't any birds or animals on it. The control tower is not located where they can see the runway very well.*

The Major and I have come a long way to bonefish para-dise—Christmas Island (Kiritimati), Republic of Kiribati. We land and taxi to a stop. We sit; we wait. Nothing happens. Silence. After several minutes a rear door pops open. Forty of us wait in anxious silence. We occupy but a fraction of the plane's carrying capacity. Most of the forward hull has been converted to cargo space to tote perishable food, cases of soda pop, beer, and dry goods such as cloth from which islanders make clothes; today a new pickup truck is aboard. Christmas Island does not produce finished goods or even much food except some vegetables and fruit, poultry, pork, coconut and, of course, lots of fish. Air Marshall Islands' once-a-week flight is the atoll's only timely transportation link with major sup-pliers in Hawaii, 1300 miles north. Tarawa, Kiribati's capital, is the next closest resource base; it rests 1500 miles west.

73

A young Gilbertese in faded red shirt, black pants and surgeon's mask enters by the rear door. Marching forward quick-time, he sprays a mist across the cabin. Then, opening the cargo hatch door, he hops nimbly over its foot high sill and is gone. One wag among us utters, "Good heavens, do you suppose they think we're contaminated? At least there shouldn't be any flies on the island." We all laugh. But the laugh is more from nervousness than humor. We want out and most of us do not know exactly what to expect when we get out. Some have been here before. They smile patiently.

After retrieving baggage from a bedraggled wood arrivals shed, we mob the immigration, agriculture, fisheries and customs people. Mass confusion on a small scale! The customs' man is astounded when I declare no liquor or tobacco. He looks with bureaucratic seriousness and some disgust into my sanitized luggage. No duty to collect here. What a shame!

Transport to the Captain Cook Hotel is by a traditional old yellow school bus that wears MERRY CHRISTMAS EXPRESS over its destination sign. Clumps of coconut trees greet us as we trail an indelicate pall of black diesel smoke past the village of Banana. It is a collection of palm thatched, sagging sheet metal and wood shacks bunched together on tan-gray earth pounded rock-hard by generations of bare feet. Brown people lounge and puff cigarettes as if this is some kind of movie set. Our driver honks often and the people wave. Everyone smiles. Bushes and dwarfed trees all along the highway are festooned with beer cans—*Fosters* silver and blue, *Heineken* green, black and silver, *Budweiser* red, white and blue. Well, after all, this is Christmas Island and perhaps these are Christmas trees.

The Captain Cook Hotel is a set of interconnected cement blockhouse structures that encompass sun and salt-bleached cobblestone weedy courtyards. Its half dozen palm thatch-roofed bungalows guard the beach and overlook an amber reef pool, crashing surf froth and peacock blue ocean. Wild camellias and their soft perfume are everywhere. One flowering tree, the size and shape of a mature oak but whose name I don't know, is resplendent with tiny, vivid yellow and orange blooms.

As we unpack in our bungalow, I look onto the beach grass courtyard to see several hens and a rooster parading through—probably Rhode Island Reds. They scatter like so many chicken feathers as a pounding herd of six great brown, tan and dirty-white hogs beats its way toward the beach. I learn later these are semi-domesticated critters raised for food. They use their powerful long snouts to burrow in damp coral sand just above the tide line. They must be searching for crabs, except that I have never heard of crab-eating pigs. No doubt one of these porkers will be featured fare at our luau.

We rig fly rods and rush to the courtyard—ready for fish. That we have been up since two in the morning is no deterrent. Adrenaline waxes as we bounce on benches in the back of a derelict yellow Datsun pickup—out to fish Arthur Flat under the supervision of John, guide for the day. The twisty hardpan road we travel among coconut palms is filled with humps and bumps. Our fly rods, hung in wood racks suspended on wires six inches or so below a plywood roof that covers the truck's bed, take a terrible beating on this jolting ride. Occasionally a palm frond smacks the cab top with a "crack" and bangs along the truck's roof supports. We dodge and shudder, wondering when a rod will be destroyed.

Firm, cream, two foot deep flats extend hundreds of yards out to where they meet the coral drop-off into lime-green water. The water is transparent—at least it seems so. In no time at all John, our guide, is telling me to strip long and slow, then to stop, then to quick-strip once. He acts like a fish is following my fly and my thought is that this guy is putting me on. Not so. There is a hard strike and I give my good old steel-head yank. The fish is gone. Drats! John looks over his shoulder at me, "No have to pull so hard. Just easy. Use strip set. You know how? Fish set hook when he swim."

It's the Major's turn now and soon John has him into a fish. The Major is dancing and yelling that he has a bone, he has a bone. But alas, immodesty leads to a good dunking as his feet slip from under him, his peach-shirted arms flail. Suddenly he is playing the bone from a sitting position, his chin six inches above water level. Still, he holds the fly rod and reel high and splutters at me not to report this embarrassment to the *Blue Dun Fly Shop* crowd at home. Bill Barnett, affectionately known as "the Major," Wenatchee's professor Emeritus of real estate development and fly fishing, is playing a fish from the seat of his pants! The fish is caught and released as are many others. But neither of us "see" any of the fish we cast to and that is disconcerting—because the flats' water seems absolutely clear. John sees the fish but we do not—at least not yet.

That evening as we sip cold drinks in the Maneaba, a huge, open air, thatch roofed common area, the Major is in fine fettle. He has not only caught a bonefish, he has caught several. He announces to all that the trip is already a success. But he is considerably less effusive as he eyes our dinner of baked trevally and boiled rice. One poke with his fork at the sticky rice causes him to remark that he never has cared much for Le Page's glue. The ever-present coconut bread and rolls are no compensation!

From across the mess hall comes crackling and snapping. Electric sparks? Sure enough. Next to and above the coffee making machine there is a two foot by four foot screened apparatus cut into the wall. Hot bulbs are inside and scores of house flies are drawn into the heat where they explode. "Guess that spray on the plane doesn't work very well. Either that or these flies have got a long flight range," remarks one of our table mates. The weary crew wends its way toward a good night's sleep.

Prevailing easterly trades carry soft breeze and gentle surf rumble to cool us and lull us to sleep. Every morning we are awakened in the dark about six by eerie shrieks from an invisible gecko that lives in our ceiling. Perhaps this is a Gilbertese alarm clock.

Today we travel by truck to London Village, a cluster of dilapidated sheet metal and palm huts fronted by smoky cooking fires and relaxed locals. One chap is walking the road with a large dressed-out pig draped across his shoulders—perhaps that is our dinner. The dock area is home to several motorized punts and an outrigger all painted fire engine red. You can always tell who's fished out of London Village on a given day— just take a look at the angler's pants' seat! Our trip to the flats this morning is by outrigger with its puffing, halting outboard. Something is wrong with the motor's liquid cooling system, but our story-telling, guffawing, carefree guides are immune to such nuisances. They're eating breakfasts of cold fish and rice piled high on aluminum plates while Major Bill shudders.

Tyrone, today's guide, tells Bill to cast 40 feet at eleven o'clock. The cast is true. "Stroke, long slow stroke, again, stop, short strip, short strip, stop," from Tyrone and the fish is on—a big one taking all the fly line and running off a hundred yards of backing in a nanosecond. I cast blind and have a vicious strike. My fish, races Bill's for a coral outcrop, bends around Bill and our lines cross. Bill ducks and twists away from entrapment and a possible garroting while Tyrone and I yell conflicting directions at him. He is pirouetting on one foot in belly deep water like some deranged ballet dancer—no dunking today. Both of us are savvy enough to hold our rods high over our heads to keep the fish up off the coral ledge. The fish

tire and are at hand. They are seven pounders and as we attempt to photograph them, Tyrone manhandles one and loses it. These guides land fish by grabbing the leader and hauling the fish from the water.

Tyrone hangs his head in disgrace and pulls his T-shirt over his face as Bill and I chuckle that there will be more fish. "Don't worry, be happy," I croon to an embarrassed Tyrone.

There is a good reason for my relaxed attitude. We are fishing a pancake flat—a raised coral sand beach surrounded by water and rock coral—with big hungry easy to hook bonefish everywhere. Even blind casts into waist deep water elicit strikes. The Major fixes me with his steely eyes and mutters, "I don't see what's so hard about this. You'd think from all those bonefish books that a guy would have to be an eagle-eyed casting champ. Humph! So much for the books. I'm glad I read yours instead of buying one myself." The tide has risen to chest level—so arm in arm we march back to the outrigger. Now is no time to fall in.

Over sushi and drinks served that evening in the Maneaba, a lady who fished near us today and saw us slamming bones asks, "Well, how many fish did you and Bill catch? It must have been a forty fish day for you two." I stumble badly in reply, muttering that I don't know because we don't count our catch. She is perplexed and may suspect me of dissembling. "I don't see your names on the board for tomorrow's fishing. I 'spose you two pros are going to some secret spot." The eyes of our table mates are upon me and I shock them to the quick.

We will not fish tomorrow. We'll walk the beach—spend a day in camp, take it easy. All conversation halts except, "Not fishing? Why would you come all this way, spend all that money, and not fish? How are you going to get your fair share?" More questions—some spoken and some implicit in the astonished eyes around me. All I can think to say is, "How much is enough? How many bonefish would make you happy? Bill and I don't know the number, but I guess we made it. That's all I know about a fair share." It passes through my mind that they think me to be deranged. Time for escape. Time to go to the luau to meet a porker acquaintance in a new guise!

Today the Major and I are beachcombing—collecting shells for our ever-patient wives. Sun-bleached sea urchins, pastel purple, pearl bejeweled in gray skirts, geometric mysteries of perfect symmetry, are prizes. Multitudes of minute conch-like shells in browns and purples are everywhere; each shell is home to a tiny, fairy-like crab; and, almost every crab has an outer skin that is cream hued with strong slices of brilliant orange/red definition on elbow joints. Having noticed these crabs early in our trip, I created a fly—known around camp as Paul's Perfect Orange Blossom—because it imitates the crabs' body and definition colors. Bonefish devour it.

At lunch in the mess hall we are alone under the slowly turning wood paddle fans until a lithe young cocoa-skinned woman enters and asks if she may join us. We have seen her around camp and are glad to have her company. The Major is enthralled. He doffs his *Blue Dun* hat and ushers her to a seat beside him. She wonders why we are not fishing and we tell her that we are taking a day off to rest and walk the island. She makes no bones about her feelings. She is totally disgusted with this place. "My room is full of ants, those damned crabs are so thick outside that you have to watch everywhere you go, there's nothing to do here but fish. I can't even go shopping. If I'd known what this island was like, I'd never have accepted the assignment!"

She says she is a professional escort and has come here with a wealthy Asian entrepreneur who thought he might be lonesome. At dinner on their first night, he insisted that she cut his fish entrée and she refused. Things have gone from bad to worse and now they are not speaking. She refers to him contemptuously as a "sissy man" because he cannot tie on his own flies, and complains constantly about walking the flats and being tired. In obvious naiveté I ask her what an escort actually does. Bill, of course, is sitting there with a pizza plate grin waiting for her to smack me. But no such luck for pal Bill.

She explains in deep dulcet tones that her services include conversation and providing pleasant company for her employers. In this work she has met interesting people and enjoyed free travel to sundry exotic places. She pays no federal or state income taxes on her earnings. As the Major and I depart the mess hall and enter blistering sunshine, he removes his cap, peers at me and in daft incredulity utters, "Can you imagine that? She doesn't pay income tax?" I think to myself, "Well, Major, you've finally met your match."

Fishing takes us to creamy flats with splendid names. There is Go Like Hell, Nine Mile, Elena, Arthur, Rick's, Smoking, Y-site, Lone Pine, Paris and one other that Tyrone has named Paul's Point. We wade warm shallows, keen-eyed for those gray-green lightning streaks that illumine imagination. We begin "to see" fish and make some very good casts, "bean" plenty of fish and agree to blame the damn' wind for "beanings" and all other errant casts. Fishing is so good that I tell Bill, "Those guys who write the books about how you have to cast eighty feet to reach a bone and about how hard they are to catch must be trying to impress someone. Whada yuh 'spose they smoke for lunch?"

Most of our success is attributable to Tyrone who we have hired as our permanent guide. He is a joy. Stubby and chocolate brown with a great mop of black thatch, he does a bouncing dance-step on the flats' coral sand, blows great pink bubble gum bubbles, hums folk tunes, laughs to himself, sways his arms as if conducting an invisible chorus. He is searching, always searching—hoping to get us into the "beeg" fish. A sharp-eyed stalker, he is almost always on the move. "See dat fly. Tyrone da barber give him haircut. Dat jus' right. You gonna get a beeg, beeg fish. You see. Les' go. " So the days pass.

Tomorrow is plane day for Bill and we are sitting in our thatched bungalow—sipping day's end drinks, guffawing at inconsequential events, while giving his gear a thorough cleaning. Easterlies are crashing and roaring on the reef, bringing welcome breezes to us. Yet I am still wondering, "Major, I 'spose I stepped in it again the other night. They didn't like what I said about a fair share. What's a fair share to you? Can you do any better than I did?"

The Major slouches on his cot, *Blue Dun Fly Shop* hat perched on his uncut locks. Indeed, he has developed shapely white curls all down his neck because it has been so long since his last hair cut. His long-sleeved peach-pink tropical fishing shirt shows a dried chalky watermark across its chest—commemorative of that first afternoon's dunking. His beloved wife Jo will not have much laundry to do when the Major arrives at her doorstep.

"Well, it's not a number. At least it's not a number I know anything about. Maybe a fair share is a chance, an opportunity for a trip, a sighting, a cast—a hookup rather than an endup. Know what I mean? It's more about trying than getting. Sure, it's good to get. I love to catch fish. But maybe real joy is in the dream and hope and then having a chance to try. Course that's hard to explain to most people. One thing I know for sure. I've had my fair share in this life!" He punctuates all of that with a last draught of his Crown Royal. He has exquisite taste!

Plane day for the Major comes too soon for me. But he's eager to be on his way home — then to a beloved spring creek hidden away in Montana's Bitterroot solitude. It is where that loner, bruiser brown lives, the one that always comes to the Major's favorite fly — the #14 Royal Wulff.

ANOTHER TIME

Clatter and commotion ebb. Another band of anglers board the MERRY CHRISTMAS SPECIAL to catch their outgoing flight. Some have told me they are grateful to be leaving. "There is something," they say, "about this island's isolation that seems forbidding. It's too far away." As I sit on the Mane-aba beach, watching far off purple ocean swells, waiting for Tyrone and a ride to London, I wonder, "Too far away from what? Cities? Stores? Heaven help us — freeways?" Who knows? Caressing melodies born eons ago in places beyond imagination are on the air. Warm sea-scent blesses me. Breakers run in off the reef and turn over on themselves only to disappear and be replaced by others — an endless cycle. I am absolutely alone and contented — basking in morning sun. But not for long!

An enthusiastic new crew arrives and in no time four of us pack off to London in a yellow, rust-bucket pickup. Two folks, husband and wife, introduce themselves as "New Yawkas," and I am intrigued. They are dressed like Orvis models and each wears one jade earring from a matched set. Surely this cannot be — not among fly fishers. Tyrone studies them carefully. They address each other as "honey." Apparently Tyrone has never heard this form of address before because he frowns at its use. The husband looks to be fifty and the wife twenty two. Tyrone stares entranced. Another angler in our party wears a heavy camouflage duck hunter's parka; surely he is not serious.

Moon and tide are perfect for fishing Paris today; bonefish abound. Almost immediately upon entering the water, Mr.

Camouflage, who has never hooked a fast fish before, hits a flats burner. Attempting to land a "green" fish too quickly, he is entangled and lassoed by his desperate adversary. Mr. C. wails for assistance but is ignored because everyone is busy. *"A voice crying out in the wilderness,"* I chuckle. But now comes the real fun.

A giant trevally of more than a hundred pounds glides from deep water onto the flat, moving languorously among us like a tamed, fearless, aquarium specimen. The "New Yawka's" wife shouts for him to cast to the fish. Mr. "New Yawka" lunges and twists with his 12-weight—not much of a caster. Not much luck attracting the fish either and I turn away. My business is to land a bonefish that Tyrone claims will weigh ten pounds.

As we work the fish, Tyrone questions me about men who wear earrings. He giggles, "Why he call her honey? What kind of person honey? You call you wife honey? Put honey on bread wid peanut butter. Honey sweet. Wife no sweet. Dat right? Why he say dat?" I chuckle and tell Tyrone that some people call their beloved, "honey." He nods as if in understanding, wraps his arm around my shoulders and directs. "You catch 'um deese fish quick. Beeg, beeg bonefish coming. You cast to 'um."

Havoc! Immense crashing and splashing; screams of delight and fear. The giant trevally has been hooked and is headed for Tarawa. All the fly line is gone and then an awful lot of backing disappears from our companion's Abel 4 reel. I wonder why the "New Yawka" is not holding his rod tip high to keep the fish out of coral heads. But no, his rod is parallel to the surface—and that is the end of that. Fly line and lots of backing are lost. He spends a shaky morning wondering where he can find another fly line and why the guide did not remind him to keep his rod tip high. Great morning of fishing! But it's time to move; Tyrone has plans.

The big motor is sick again. No water is coming from its water cooling system outlet and I tell Tyrone to have the boatman shut it down before it burns out. In his basso profundo Tyrone gives proper instructions and we plod along with the fifteen horse motor—barely making steerage. Standing in the prow with headwind blowing over and around me, facing the lagoon's deep green and blue and the distant islets' lemon and gold, I have a feeling of profound freedom and well-being. I belong here.

My five ounce steelhead baitcasting rod, with a nine inch blue and white jointed plug, is rattling around. Might as well troll in our backwash, we're certainly moving slowly enough. Damn motor! Surprise! The crew's rollicking gab and laughter is interrupted by a heavy take and overpowering long run. "Turn us around. Turn us around. Follow the fish." More runs, as I pump and reel, pump and reel. Steelhead rods and fifteen pound monofilament lines are not made for such bullying.

But I am lucky and after forty five minutes, an iridescent silver and blue glow appears, drifting up from turquoise depths— a wahoo comes to boat side. As Tyrone grabs hold of the wire shock leader, I turn away. We have no net or gaff and I cannot bear to watch him lose the fish. But behold, a miracle! The huge, long fish is dragged up over the punt's four foot side. Nothing breaks and we have it. The plug's rear #4/0 hook is crushed; it's blue head is scarred white with a deep cut. By golly, I kind of like this junker motor!

After the fish is measured and pictures are taken, Tyrone moves from his position aft to sit beside me. "What you do wid deese fish?" he wants to know. "Oh, I'll take it back to camp. They'll cook it or make sushi. I like sushi." Tyrone stares at me with imploring brown eyes. He is disappointed. I know what he wants, but I am going to play him like a fish and so I say no more. Not a word. Melancholy, Tyrone returns to his perch and silent companions—the boatman, assistant boatman and two guides. A few sad comments are exchanged. These are not the best of times for Tyrone and company.

A morose crew drops Tyrone and me at an area I haven't seen before. We stand knee-deep in a forty foot wide channel that parallels the beach for fifty yards. It is edged with coral heads on the lagoon side and a coral shelf on the beach side. Scudding clouds create shadows that make fish spotting difficult. Howling wind off the lagoon creates a lime-chalk wave wash. Bad clouds, bad wind, bad water. I wonder if Tyrone has placed me here as a punishment!

Shadows flit ten feet in front of us in fifteen inches of thick chalk-wash. They are large bonefish unaware of our presence. Tyrone gives frantic casting directions. But the best I can do is clumsy thirty foot slap casts. Under normal circumstances such blunders would cause a fish stampede, but not today. Still, casting to butterflies in a gale is not my forte.

So I make a blind cast—then a long, slow stroke. Stop. Short stroke. Short stroke. Zip! The fish come with savage strikes. Big fish. Mostly, their violent runs take them into coral on one side or the other where my fifteen pound Maxima pops. When I hold too tightly or get tangled, they straighten a #4 Mustad hook. The air is filled with terns plucking at me and my rod tip. They are trying to drive us away from their nearby beach nesting area. This is a crazy place. I love it. I love fishing blind in this wind. We fish until the incoming tide drives us out. This is where I belong all right!

Back in the punt, Tyrone hovers over our grand wahoo. With soulful, pleading eyes, he tells me that the people back at camp will not appreciate the fish as much as his family. Besides, he will divide the fish with our boatmen and guides. Tyrone is eloquent; the other Gilbertese follow his delivery with rapt attention. All wait with longing expressions. You'd think that their well-rounded bellies were wasted away with famine. After a long pause as if in deep thought, I agree that Tyrone may have the fish. He grunts acceptance in his deep bass voice as if he is doing me a favor. The issue is settled.

As we return toward London Harbor, the water beneath us blooms suddenly with multitudes of porpoises whose gleaming silver-brown bottle-like shapes ricochet up and down from blue depths to green shallows and from side to side in sparkling flashes. They race us and then fall behind and then speed toward our harbor destination to disappear without so much as a surface tremor. It has been a good day, good fishing. "Verah good fishing."

All the camp's inhabitants have gone fishing this morning. Their palm thatched bungalows stand like abandoned sentinels watching over a still courtyard and paths. It is too early for cleaning ladies or yard workers to be out. As I walk by the closed mini-mart store front, hens and their rooster peck for invisible morsels. A skinny flea-bitten black cat licks her dirty albino kitten. They nestle in the store's doorway—probably waiting for a handout—not very prosperous looking scavengers.

Morning takes me on a several mile beach hike past enormous colonies of shallow water sea urchins with their shiny black spiny backs. Many have been washed high up on the sand where they dried and sun-faded to faint purple and white; their rounded surfaces are of delicate ridges and clefts that form elegant, simple, flawless patterns—identical from one shell to another—the geometry of a divine artisan.

The beach is well endowed with what I call the Dalmatian shells. An inch or so around, they are conch-like with black spots arranged in precise bands on an enameled white surface; their patterns are like those of hand-woven Indian baskets I have seen in Arizona. Purple coral pieces shaped just like blackboard chalk are strewn everywhere. The great cream beach is a world of pastels—purple, pink, orange, and faded carmine and brown.

Occasionally I see indistinct stick-figure silhouettes far ahead. Some stand by the reef pool and cast hand nets; others move among the palms, perhaps to gather copra or firewood. All vanish as mirages before I reach them. Walks here remind me of the Cape Cod beach. But the Cape beach, though sometimes wild and lonely, is close to its populated land-mass; it is not a lonesome place. This atoll is a faded green flotsam speck adrift among menacing blue-black oceanic swells—lost in a arcane pelagic universe, close to nowhere. Such isolation causes some to be uncomfortable on the atoll. Strange to say, I have never seen another angler, except the Major, walk this wondrously decorated shelf. That's all right. I'll keep it for myself.

Back in camp, cleaning ladies are at work. Rotund with black hair tied back in buns, they wear faded yellow smocks and shuffle along in flip-flops, never raising a foot more than an inch or so above ground. Smiling to themselves they blow gum bubbles and sing or whistle, calling constantly to each other in high cheerful bird-like tones. Two men with straw brooms are sweeping the beach near our bungalow. I have studied them carefully for days and never figured out just what it is they sweep away. They, too, chew bubble gum and chat endlessly.

Lots of chores for me to do in the bungalow today—fly lines and reels are rinsed with drinking water taken from the refrigerator; the tap water is brackish. Shorts and shirts are washed and rinsed in tap water and hung to dry in the sun on a monofilament clothesline. No matter how long they remain there, they will come off just a bit sticky with salt and damp— smelling faintly of Palmolive soap. Trivia consumes my day and delights me. Peace and quiet. Perhaps I'll tie up some George Bushes after a while. Ah, solitude and a snooze....

"Bang. Bang." The screen door slaps and rattles. Tyrone has arrived, eyes bugging with excitement. "We fish tomorrow? Verah good skinny water. You favorite. I know. We fish all day. Verah, verah good." He's right. I love the skinny water best of all. Let's hope for lots of sun, no clouds and a little

88

wind. It is agreed. The two of us will spend the day on skinny water—in places secret from the atoll's other anglers.

Tyrone stomps off with my last Fosters beer murmuring to himself, "Fishing be verah good tomorrow, verah good. Big Bad Tyrone the Ladies' man show you." Clomping across the weed-thick courtyard, he slows and enters his bounce-step. His arms come up gently so that he is beating time for his dance and chorus troupe—the Fosters is his baton. Tyrone is happy, "verah happy." Goats that have replaced yesteryear's porkers dodge the absent-minded musician.

Skinny water bonefish! But Tyrone and I have a long walk from our punt to the fish and so he introduces his favorite new topic. Next year when I return, he wants me to stay at the hotel in London. He will cook for me and we will use his father's boat so that we can fish anywhere we want. Of course Tyrone will collect the total guide fee rather than splitting it with the Captain Cook. To me the shambles of tin and palm thatch he calls a hotel looks like "hepatitis house." The thought of eating cold fish and rice for a couple of weeks causes my stomach to churn. Fancy the specter—Tyrone in an apron. I could become permanently damaged! At last we've reached our destination—no more discussion.

The flat is immense and of clean coral sand with six inches of water that breaks sharply over bush-like coral into green depths. Water is running off the flat and slightly towards us. Bonefish are tail-to-us and laying parallel with the beach. They rest in small sand troughs midst wave wash, waiting for flats tidbits to be swept to them. The fly must be cast above and parallel to the fish so that the tide drifts it to the fish well ahead of the fly line. Timing is everything and a good reach cast is required. I crawl to approach our targets—intense and casting well. Tyrone giggles—pleased with my accurate casts. One George Bush after another is shredded. I'm learning.

What good luck! Ahead, we see a foot-deep streamlet running off the shallow flat—like a flats spring creek. Fish hang in a tide-dug pocket just where stream-flow enters green water. To get near enough to cast but not frighten the fish, I have to duck-walk fifty feet along the beach shelf, with waves lapping pretty close to my chin and coral heads shaving along my bottom. A reach cast bent right takes George Bush to a fish that sizzles with surface-cutting dorsal back up the creek, and almost onto the beach. Going. Going. Pop! Gone. Is this living!

Several times after the tide has swept George past a stubborn bonefish and into the green, a small trevally charges good old George and breaks him among coral heads. One nice bone speeds off the flat, over coral heads and into the green only to return like a bullet straight at us. A door-sized trevally in hot pursuit bursts onto the flat crashing and splashing not five feet in front of us and then is gone, leaving with a big chunk of bonefish flesh. "Too bad you pull too soon. Maybe catch trevally on bonefish," Tyrone grins. *Sure Tyrone—on an 8-weight rod with a #6 George Bush!* I am reminded of the morning when a large black-tip shark rose to gobble up a nice bonefish I had allowed to run into deeper water. To my anguished cries Tyrone had laughed, "Humph, better he take bonefish than come eat us." *You bet Tyrone, you pill!*

True to his word, Tyrone is forcing me to fish all day today and so he whistles down the punt for a short trip to Paul's Point and Paul's Flat. We fish here when the tide is twenty inches or less of water. It is not a flat I would choose because it appears transparent and fishless with no tidal movement. But that is illusion. Countless singles and pods of jittery two to three pound fish feed in gentle tidal undercurrents. What always strikes me as ridiculous and annoying is that multitudes of fish are in clear, shallow water over a clean cream beach, but I see only a fraction of them. Tyrone is like a sorcerer whose magical power commands silvern ghosts to materialize. He points a stubby finger. "Deere." Now I see them!

How I love the flats! And it's more than the fishing and learning. It's the soft pastel texture of the place—the quiet, the seclusion and silence, the illusion of peacefulness. Warm flats water encircles and embraces me. Water music whispers in the wave wash and bathes my soul. I am enlivened and soothed—a willing captive of flats solitude—alone but not lonesome. This is a place of fantasy where magic is the practice.

Tomorrow is plane day and most folks are excited about leaving or going home. I don't know which. But I note the same anticipation every plane day eve on Christmas Island. There is something about the atoll's isolation—despite world class fishing—that makes folks uneasy. Toward dinner's end, a rumor begins to circulate among hopeful evacuees. It is as if some dread disease is abroad. "The plane may not come tomorrow."

After dinner we adjourn to the bar area. Rumor is confirmed. *The plane will not come tomorrow. Something is wrong with the plane. What could be the problem? Is the plane in Tarawa or Honolulu?* No one knows. And so island routine is broken—the "schedule" has been violated. Incredulous old men, brush-cut hair and khaki clad—some of whom are incredibly powerful in their corporate world—are impotent here. They belly up to the bar for the solace of doubles. One younger man utters a doleful, "I'm out of money. I hadn't planned on any extra time here. Doesn't anyone know when the plane will come?"

That query sets off more conversation. Palau, head guide, manager of routine and keeper of the "schedule" is questioned. But he shrugs off the questions with a wry wistful grin and quiet voice. "Plane come maybe forty eight hours, two days. It need new parts. You fish tomorrow, you tell me now, please." Palau is resigned. Sometimes the plane does not come when it is due. Once, recently, it did not come for two weeks. *Plane service can* be *irregular.* That is what they told us when we signed up to come here! So the troops march out. "Slap...Slap." The bar's screen door punctuates ended conversation.

Next morning a pall hangs over camp. Not one bungalow door is open. Even the reef's song is muted, distant and forlorn. No one is fishing today but me and, alas, Tyrone arrives in a state of disarray. He's been up all night partying. His usually neatly brushed mop of black hair is tousled, his bloodshot eyes express pain and he is massaging his stomach. Things are not good with Tyrone as he looks to heaven and moans. Nevertheless we see fish and do well at Elena. As he returns from his second trip into the bush, I ask with a malicious grin, "You all right Tyrone? Big Bad Tyrone party last night? Have a stomach ache? Too much Fosters?"

He grimaces in baleful silence. By lunch time he has consumed half a pack of Gelusel. For lunch he downs a mythical portion of cold boiled fish and rice. By three I am tired of catching skinny water fish and am ready to hang it up. To my suggestion that we quit, Tyrone grins, "One more, jus' one more." On we go. No mercy from Tyrone. "Here, you fish a while I tell him." He laughs, "Why you so tired? Drink too much Fosters!"

Two days later it is announced that the plane will come next day. Dejected, marooned souls are elated. Freedom from island bondage at last! Folks laugh and joke over drinks. "Well, we'll be back on the mainland in twenty four hours unless there's some holdup in Honolulu. Course even if we get stuck there, we can find a good steak and decent place to stay." Confidence restored, atoll servitude lifted, details of cleaning gear and packing are upon us.

For me, though, there is a gentle sadness and sense of imminent loss implicit in leaving this atoll. In part that is because I always learn so much here and will miss the source of that learning. I have sat alone in late afternoon and at night in my dimly lit room and tied bunches of Magic Orange Blossoms, piles of George Bushes and bizarre krystal flash variants. I, of three thumbs, have become sufficiently skilled at tying so as not to need a magnifier or much light. Observations of beach life have informed me and that information has been used to create imitations that fish like to eat. Through the solitary work of making flies I have learned and grown—perhaps become a little more independent! But there is more.

I have sailed Kiritimati's rich lagoon and waded its translucent flats; explored rich beaches and prowled derelict camp grounds. I have stood for hours in black beach night—always with surf sound rumbling over me—searching for that lone shooting star midst white-gold clusters and sometimes finding even more. I have spent much time alone; even on the flats with Tyrone, we've been apart more than together—each in his own world. So atoll life has become familiar and pleasurable and exciting to me. Yes, this is a lonesome place, but not lonely—at least not for me. I have found my niche here and am bonded with the atoll.

For me the island has an irresistible, sensual and emotional attraction. I see pastels dancing as chimera from reef to pool; from lagoon to flats and then splashed pink and orange and purple—formed as spidery critters and shells and exotic coral pieces—on solitary beaches. I hear humming cleaning women, whistling grounds' sweepers; growling deep-voiced Tyrone; and always wind-drifted hypnotic reef song. I inhale island scents—of smoky, smoldering village cook fires; dusty coral roads; luau broiled lobster and baked porker; and ever cleansing warm sea-scent. I taste wondrous brown-toasted lobster tails and tender pork loins washed down with Fosters—never forgetting the Major's shudder at bland trevally and gluey rice.

Beyond all those sensations is the consuming impression of ageless, almighty sea endlessly grinding and shaping and polishing its volcanic progeny—always with thunder on the air. I find all of this soothing and invigorating.

Kiritimati is where fantasy is transformed by island magic to reality. It is where land and scent and sea fill my soul with joy. I could remain here for a very long time! But—just as there are arrivals, there must be departures.

Time to go now. Time to go home.

Past Recaptured

Ages have passed since last I stood on this once so-familiar
bridge, peering into tannic flow, searching for a tell-tale turn of silver.
What have I missed? Well, as the wise ones say "That's water
under the bridge, friend, water under the bridge."

MY FOOTSTEPS seek old boot prints—peculiar impressions left by odd, aluminum-studded cleats I have worn for eons. Almost no one uses these heavy, unwieldy, old-fashioned mudsuckers anymore! But smudged muddy tracks that once crisscrossed these grass-overgrown river banks are gone—faded by time and the river. For it is six years since last I cast a line here. Still, I remember the path's twists and turns—and the best places from which to lay out a line.

Hardly anyone is fishing this morning. Just two affluent-looking younger men on the main drift who are clad in handsome green Gore-Tex parkas and brown neoprene waders. Where is the mob? Early December always brings crowds to both sides of the drift. Where is June, cigarette dribbling from lower lip, who always pouts and whose bald head steams when someone else lands a steelhead and he doesn't? Where is Harry in his stove-pipe red hat, chewing and spitting remnants of a dead cigar—forever talking, chuckling, and hopeful? Where is that nice guy from Anacortes who smokes the sweet-smelling pipe? None of the old hip-booted, plaid, wool-jacketed bunch is here. I wonder why not? No fish in yet? But that's odd. The steelhead are always here now.

There is something strange about the air on the river. I sniff and sniff. What is it? And finally it comes to me. There is no tobacco smoke hanging on the water—no cigarette and cigar and pipe haze drifting downstream from the Old 99 Bridge.

I look around for Butch, the smiling bristly-faced black lab and part something who always fishes with us. No Butch. Weird.

So December days pass. Near the I-5 bridge, paths once well-trod by steelheaders are overgrown with blackberry vines and briars—though plunkers have managed to trim nests over a few promising deep drifts. West of the bridge, where a path once edged great fishing all the way to the railroad bridge and its fabulous Chinook holding water, there is no path. Instead, an impenetrable six foot high blackberry patch has overgrown the valley bottom. Behind the Methodist church on Allen West, where steelheading used to be so good—and especially after a hard snowstorm, great thorn and alder thickets hedge once-accessible river bank. Doesn't anyone fish here anymore?

One lucky morning near the Sheep Bridge I hit a fish on my silver-bodied and fluorescent lime yarn winged bug—the one that imitates a Sammy. "Strange-looking steelhead," I mutter. "Never saw a steelhead with forked tail like that. And those black crosses on the back. Hell, that's no steelhead; it's an Atlantic salmon escaped from the commercial hatchery pens. Humph. Maybe we'll have an Atlantic salmon fishery on the Pacific Coast. The world is changing!"

A rusty red old pickup and its owner await me and my Atlantic salmon near the Sheep Bridge public parking access. "See you got one of them suckers. Good. They's a few of 'um here. Proly ruinin' the river." He is puffing a Winston while fixing up his bait casting gear and eggs for a run at the "slow drift." He talks and dresses like one of the old-timers though I don't remember him. But we get to talking and I have to ask my questions.

"June? Yeah, he died last fall of smoking. Joe from Ana-cortes? Passed away a year or so ago—'prostrate' finally got him. Harry? He's gone too. Died of something. Even ole Bob,

lived right over there is gone. Course all these guys smoked." He smiles sheepishly. "Damn, I got to quit. I'm only fifty. I still got a chance." Salt and pepper whiskered with failed black teeth and ruddy complexion shaded by a greasy John Deere cap, he is well worn.

We part with words that we'll fish together next time. "Butch?" I query. "Oh he's gone off somewhere. Haven't seen him since the big fall Chinook run. Hell they's so few silvers he's proly found hisself another place or quit for the winter! Smart cookie, that Butch. He'll be back in the fall. You kin bet on that!"

My route home is by way of Bow-Edison's Farm to Market Road. I park at the Samish River bridge and push through tall sage marsh grass to the stump pool—a hike I've taken so many times. Sure enough friend heron is there with webs barely touched by ebbing wavelets. Slate gray stone-still hunchback, he pores over a slow tannic outrun tide. Searching for.... a sculpin, or eelet or fingerling cutthroat? Who knows? But my appearance surprises him and he lurches aloft and downriver to probe other waters—*beloved waters*—his and mine.

We are forever hopeful.